Dark Psychology

From an Ex-CIA Operative Officer, Everything You Need
to Know About Covert Manipulation Techniques
& How to Protect Yourself Against Them.

Harold Fox

Hello!

Thank you for purchasing this book!

Go on www.foxharold.com or scan the QR code
to get your bonus content **"The 6 Principles of Manipulation"**
to access **limited offers** and **premium content** <u>just for you</u>!

Your friend,

Harold Fox

© Copyright Harold Fox 2021 - All rights reserved.

The content contained within this book may not be reproduced, duplicated or transmitted without direct written permission from the author or the publisher.

Under no circumstances will any blame or legal responsibility be held against the publisher, or author, for any damages, reparation, or monetary loss due to the information contained within this book. Either directly or indirectly.

Legal Notice:

This book is copyright protected. This book is only for personal use. You cannot amend, distribute, sell, use, quote or paraphrase any part, or the content within this book, without the consent of the author or publisher.

Disclaimer Notice:

By reading this document, the reader agrees that under no circumstances is the author responsible for any losses, direct or indirect, which are incurred as a result of the use of information contained within this document, including, but not limited to, — errors, omissions, or inaccuracies.

Table of Content

Introduction 1

Chapter 1: What is Dark Psychology? 5
  Regular vs. Dark Psychology 5

Chapter 2: Dark Psychology Triad 12
  Narcissism 14
    Signs of Narcissism 16
  Machiavellianism 21
    Machiavellianism Traits 25
  Psychopathy 28
    Common Signs of Psychopathy 31
  Identifying Dark Triad Traits 32
    Managing People with Dark Triad Traits 34

Chapter 3: Dark Psychology Manipulation Techniques 46
  Gaslighting 47
    How Gaslighting Happens 49
    Gaslighting and Narcissism 51
  Brainwashing 53
    Steps Used in Brainwashing 56
  Hypnosis 68
    Susceptibility 69

Induction 70
Suggestion 72
Emotional Blackmail 72
How Emotional Blackmail Works....................................... 74
Types of Emotional Blackmailing....................................... 79
Categories of Emotionally Manipulative Behavior 81

Chapter 4: The Effects of Dark Psychological Abuse 85
Cognitive Difficulties 86
Behavioral Issues 87
Emotional Problems 88

Chapter 5: Signs That You are Being Manipulated 91
Warning Signs of Gaslighting... 93
Signs of Gaslighting in Relationships 93
Signs of Gaslighting in the Workplace 97
Signs of Gaslighting Children 99
Classic Examples of Gaslighting.. 101
Questions to Ask to Know if You Are Being Gaslighted.. 105
Signs of Brainwashing 106
Signs of Hypnosis 108
Signs of Psychopathy 110
Signs of Emotional Blackmail 111
Other Indicators of Emotional Manipulation.................... 113
Signs of Manipulation in Your Friendship 114

Signs of Manipulation in Your Relationship 118
Chapter 6: Protecting Yourself Against Dark Psychology. 125
Protecting Yourself Against Narcissism 126
Protecting Yourself Against Machiavellianism 134
Protecting Yourself Against Psychopathy 137
Protecting Yourself Against Gaslighting 139
Protecting Yourself Against Brainwashing 144
Protecting Yourself Against Emotional Blackmailers 150
Conclusion 153

Introduction

As an ex-CIA operative, I was what is known as an Operations Officer, or what you might know as a "CIA Agent". As an Operations Officer, I spent most of my career serving in multi-year assignments in a variety of overseas locations. My job involved gaining certain individuals' trust and fishing for information or "intelligence" that can increase awareness of what other governments are up to. Usually, this process can take years and, oftentimes than not, lies, manipulation, and other dark psychological techniques are necessary skills needed to achieve whatever you are after.

Consider these questions: Why should an asset give you the information you seek, at the risk of their own safety and their families? What is their motivation to join your side? What benefits can you give them that surpasses their loyalty to their own country?

To answer these questions for the asset and convince them, a lot of manipulation and lies have to be employed. Sometimes, an asset might even be emotionally blackmailed so that they might comply with your wishes.

A lot of people live in denial; they assume that dark psychology does not exist or that if it does, it is not really a problem they need to deal with. However, as an ex-CIA agent, I beg to disagree; I have witnessed a lot of dark psychological manipulation to know that it exists.

Dark psychology has always been present in the world. There are always those who will search for the weaknesses in others, in order to benefit themselves. These people will use lying, persuasion, gaslighting, and other forms of manipulation to get what they want.

Believing or thinking that dark psychology does not exist has led to many people being subjugated under its influences and being taken advantage of. Granted, there are a lot of principles and ideas within the world of dark psychology. However, by learning about them, you will be able to be on the lookout for anyone who tries to use dark psychological techniques against you.

If you or anyone close to you have undergone any form of emotional trauma related to dark psychology or if perhaps you are currently experiencing the effects of dark psychology, then

I highly recommend that you read this book. Even if you have never experienced any form of dark psychology, it does not hurt to read this book so that you can be equipped with the knowledge needed to protect yourself against the nefarious practices of dark psychology. This book breaks down the complex phenomenon of dark psychology in the simplest terms – taking into consideration that you might not be familiar with any of the concepts.

Dark psychology is not a novel concept; hence, this book is not about any groundbreaking discoveries. However, there is a lot of information out there about dark psychology that is basically shrouded in barely understandable psychobabble that leaves you more perplexed than informed. Hence, this book does an effective job of demystifying dark psychology and equips you with the knowledge that you can use to protect yourself against its nefarious techniques.

The goal of this book is simple; the ultimate aim is to help you learn about dark psychology and how to protect yourself against its nefarious practices. This book contains no fluff or elaborate examples meant to fill up the pages; rather, it contains straight-to-the-point information about the various concepts discussed in this book. After reading this book, you will be able to identify the practices of dark psychology as well as ways through which you can protect yourself from such practices.

Without further ado, let us get down to it.

Chapter 1: What is Dark Psychology?

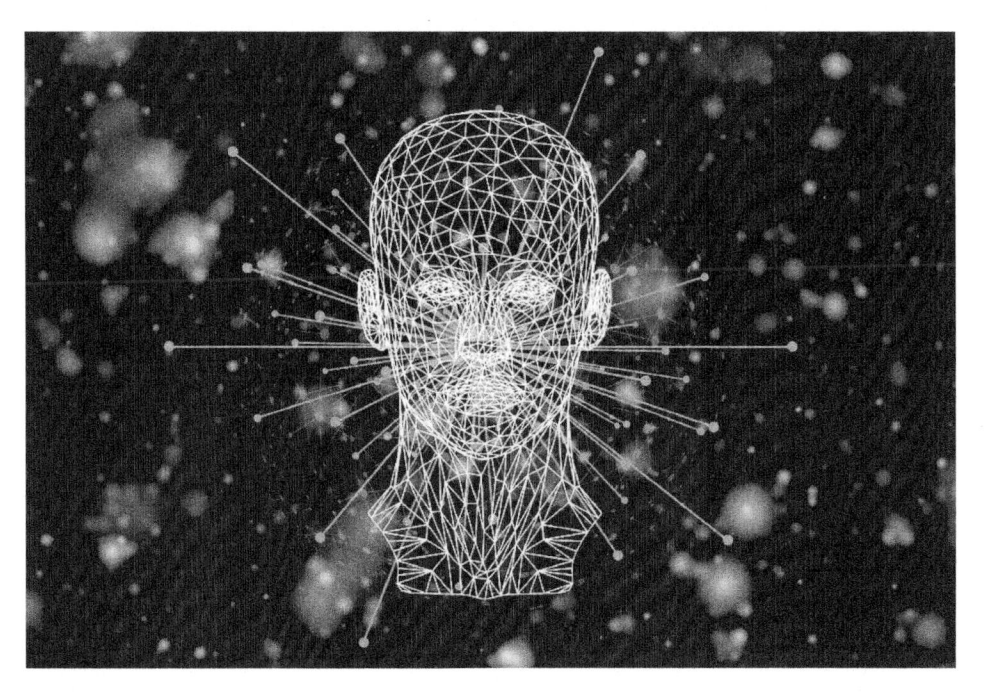

Regular vs. Dark Psychology

Basically, psychology or regular psychology is the science of mind and behavior. It refers to the study of human behavior while focusing on their actions, interactions, and thoughts.

Practitioners of regular psychology – otherwise known as psychologists – attempt to identify as well as understand the role of mental functions in individual and social behavior. At the same time, they explore the physiological and biological processes that underlie cognitive functions and behaviors. Under regular psychology, psychologists explore behavior and mental processes, including perception, cognition, attention, emotion, intelligence, subjective experiences, motivation, brain functioning, and personality. This also extends to interaction between people, such as interpersonal relationships, including psychological resilience, family resilience, and other areas.

While psychological knowledge is often applied to the assessment and treatment of mental health problems, it is also directed towards understanding and solving problems in several spheres of human activity.

Ultimately, by many accounts, psychology or regular psychology aims to benefit society. In fact, the majority of psychologists are usually involved in some kind of therapeutic role; practicing in clinical, counseling, or school settings. Many psychologists also conduct scientific research on a wide range of topics related to mental processes and behavior, and they typically work in university psychology departments or teach in other academic settings – such as medical schools and hospitals. Some psychologists, on the other hand, are employed in industrial and organizational settings, or in other areas such as human development and aging, sports, health, and the media, as well as in forensic investigation and other aspects of the law.

Conclusively, as you can see, regular psychology aims to benefit society at large.

Dark Psychology, on the other hand, is the science and art of mind control and manipulation. It refers to the study of the human condition in relation to the psychological nature and innate capacity of people to prey on other people. We all have the potential to victimize other people as well as other living creatures. While many of us tend to restrain or sublimate this tendency, some people willingly choose to act upon these impulses.

Therefore, the aim of dark psychology, as an academic field of study, involves trying to understand those feelings, thoughts and perceptions that leads to an outburst of predatory behavior that negates the contemporary understandings of human behavioral psychology.

As I mentioned earlier, we all have the potential for predatory behaviors. We have, at one time or another, had certain feelings or thoughts of behaving brutally against our fellow human beings. If you can be frank with yourself, you will agree that you have had thoughts and feelings of wanting to commit atrocious acts against other people or perhaps even animals. Given the fact that we consider ourselves as a benevolent species; one would like to believe that these dark thoughts and feelings would be non-existent in our psyche. Unfortunately, they do exist. We all have these thoughts and/or feelings, but luckily, most of us never act upon them.

However, just because you and I do not act on these impulses does not mean others do not or will not. In fact, there are people who act on these predatory behaviors without doing so for power, money, sex, retribution, or any other known purpose – they simply commit horrid acts without a goal. These are people who violate and injure others just for the sake of doing so.

Conclusively, while regular psychology tends to or aims to benefit society at large, dark psychology on the other hand tends to be self-interested and destructive to society.

The more you can visualize dark psychology, the better you would be prepared to reduce your chances of being victimized by human predators. Before proceeding to the subsequent chapters of this book, it is important for you to have at least a minimal comprehension of dark psychology. The following are three basic principles necessary for you to know so as to fully grasp the concept of dark psychology:

1. Dark psychology is not a formal branch of psychology; rather, it is basically psychology that is used abusively to achieve a harmful end. Dark psychology is basically a tool for manipulative practices; therefore, anyone that uses influence and/or persuasion in a way that harms another individual is a dark psychologist.

2. Dark psychology presupposes that everyone has the capacity for psychological violence. It is an innate potential in all humans; however, various internal as

well as external factors increase the probability for this potential to erupt into volatile behaviors. Dark psychological behaviors are predatory in nature, and can sometimes erupt without reason. Also, the phenomenon of dark psychology is solely a human occurrence and is shared by no other living creature. Although violent behavior exists in other living organisms, human beings are the only species that has the potential to execute violent behaviors without purpose. Thus, everyone you come in contact with has the potential to exhibit dark psychological behaviors. The most benevolent, compassionate, and altruistic people you know have felt the dark impulse, had the dark thoughts, but a greater number of them never act upon these impulses.

3. Dark psychology refers to the art of people using manipulative tactics such as gaslighting, brainwashing, hypnosis, and emotional blackmail just to achieve their selfish desires.

As a former law-enforcement agent who has experienced as well as utilized dark psychology in my day-to-day activities, it is my goal to educate you by increasing your self-awareness and inspiring you to educate others to embark upon the path of learning so as to reduce the probability of falling victim to those possessed by the forces explored by dark psychology.

If you have ever been a victim of a dark psychology guided predator, do not feel humiliated, we have all experienced some form of victimization at one point or another in our lives. This is why I took it upon myself to write this book so as to show you everything you need to know about dark psychology as well as how to protect yourself against it. Learning and understanding the nefarious techniques and practices of dark psychology will enable you to be able to recognize, diagnose, and protect yourself from its influences.

Chapter 2: Dark Psychology Triad

Now that you know what dark psychology is, it is time to move a little bit deeper into personality traits that define dark psychology. You see, dark psychology is not a single, universally applicable medical diagnosis that can be applied across all cases of deviant personalities. There are, in fact, a wide variety of ways that dark psychology may manifest itself in someone's psychological and behavioral makeup. These ways are divided into three broad categories, namely:

- Narcissism
- Machiavellianism

- Psychopathy

The above-mentioned categories form what is known as the Dark Triad.

All three Dark Triad traits are conceptually distinct although empirical evidence shows them to be overlapping. However, whether similar or distinct, they are all associated with a callous-manipulative interpersonal style. Sometimes, many deviant personalities with prominent features of dark psychology may display elements of more than one manifestation of dark psychology. That is to say, a narcissist may also display elements of Machiavellianism or psychopathy.

Basically, narcissism involves grandiosity, egotism, and a distinct lack of empathy while Machiavellianism is the use of manipulation to exploit and deceive people with no sense of morality. Psychopathy, on the other hand, is characterized by continuous antisocial behavior, impulsivity, selfishness, callous and unemotional traits, and remorselessness.

Let us take a deeper look at each personality trait so that you can easily identify them when you come across them.

Narcissism

The term "narcissism" originates from an ancient Greek myth about a hunter named Narcissus. According to the myth, the young man saw his reflection in a pool of water, fell in love with the image of himself, and subsequently drowned.

In clinical psychology, narcissism as an illness was introduced by Sigmund Freud and has continually been included in official diagnostic manuals as a description of a specific type of psychiatric personality disorder.

In dark psychology, narcissism is a condition characterized by an exaggerated sense of importance, an excessive need for attention, a lack of empathy, and, as a result, dysfunctional relationships. Commonly, narcissists may outwardly display an extremely high level of confidence, but this is a façade that usually hides a very fragile ego and a high degree of sensitivity to criticism.

A narcissist usually has a highly favorable view of himself or herself – resulting in an expectation that other people should extend to him or her favors and special treatment. However, when people fail to do so, the disappointment usually leads to problems that can affect all areas of the narcissist's life, including personal relationships, professional relationships, as well as financial matters.

As part of the Dark Triad, people who exhibit traits resulting from Narcissistic Personality Disorder (NPD) may engage in relationships characterized by a lack of empathy. For instance, a narcissist may demand constant comments, attention, and admiration from his or her partner, but will often appear unable or unwilling to reciprocate by displaying concern or responding to the concerns, thoughts, and feelings of his or her partner.

Furthermore, narcissists also display a sense of entitlement and expect excessive reward and recognition, but usually without ever having accomplished or achieved anything that would justify such feelings. There is also a tendency to dish out excessive criticism to those surrounding them while being extremely sensitive when the slightest amount of criticism is directed at them.

While narcissism in popular culture is often used as a pejorative term and an insult aimed at people like actors, models, and other celebrities who display high degrees of self-love and satisfaction, NPD is actually a psychological term that is quite distinct from merely having high self-esteem. The key to understanding this aspect of dark psychology is that the narcissist's image of himself or herself is often completely and entirely idealized, grandiose, and inflated and cannot be justified with any factual, meaningful accomplishments or capacities that may make such claims believable. As a result of this discord between expectation and reality, the demanding, manipulative, inconsiderate, self-centered, and arrogant behavior of the narcissist can cause problems not only for himself or herself but for all of the people in his or her life.

Basically, narcissistic people can be selfish, boastful, arrogant, devoid of empathy, and hypersensitive to criticism.

Signs of Narcissism

There are numerous signs of narcissism, most of which are quite subtle. Hence, I decided to mention a couple of signs that are usually dead-giveaway for anyone with narcissistic tendencies. The following signs can help you determine if a person is narcissistic in nature.

- **Absence of empathy:** A common sign of a narcissistic individual is a total absence of empathy. Narcissists, due to their nature, are unable to feel any iota of empathy and this is one of the main reasons why they can hurt the people around them without any sign of remorse. Also, oftentimes than not, the lack of empathy is a major reason a relationship with a narcissist fails. In a healthy relationship, both partners are meant to care for each other's well-being. However, reverse is the case in a narcissistic relationship; usually, the caring partner does not feel cared for and therefore will start to show signs of sadness and loneliness which eventually leads to the breakdown of the relationship.

- **Inflated sense of self-importance:** It is no secret that narcissists tend to have an inflated sense of self-importance. Their grandiose sense of self-importance leads them to solely concentrate on themselves thereby leaving neither time nor space for their partner or anyone else. The end result of this is that their partners are usually left feeling lonely and ignored.

- **Manifestations of arrogant and superior attitude:** Due to their inflated sense of self-importance, narcissists are probably the most arrogant human beings on the planet. They tend to act as if they are the only thing that matters in the entire universe; hence, they feel that people around them should worship them without fail.

- **Demanding excessive admiration:** If your partner is constantly fishing for compliments, or demanding admiration in other forms, then they might be a classic narcissist. Narcissists tend to demand excessive admiration up to the point that you may feel exhausted looking for new ways to express admiration for them. Even after demanding excessive admirations, they usually find it difficult to display any form of admiration for their partners. In fact, you may receive little to no compliments or admiration no matter how hard you try. And when a narcissist eventually compliments you, it is usually followed by a put-down. For instance, a narcissist might say something like "That gown looks nice but pink is not your color."

- **Little or no friends:** It is common for narcissists to have little or no friends. This is because they usually have a hard time making close connections as their narcissistic tendencies tend to push potential friends away. As a result of this, they tend to have little to no friends. Hence, because they have no friends, they usually resort to berating your friends, telling you not to spend time with them, or try to make you feel guilty for spending time with friends.

- **Feeling entitled:** Just as I mentioned earlier, due to an inflated sense of importance, narcissists expect to receive special treatment from the people around them. They think that they are extremely special; hence, they tend to act out if you do not agree with their wishes or demands. Failing to carry out their wishes and demand might lead to you receiving the "silent treatment" or "cold shoulder". Alternatively, they might throw temper tantrums or resort to name-calling or even physical abuse.

- **Demonstration of manipulative behavior:** A narcissist is an expert at manipulations – especially emotional manipulations. A narcissist favorite form of manipulation is gaslighting, where they try to cause feelings of confusion, low self-esteem, anxiety, shame, and guilt in you. A narcissist might try to control your thoughts and desires, they might manipulate you to stay away from friends and family, stay away from work, engage in obscene sexual acts, or even extort money from you. Basically, anyone that tries to force you into doing something you do not want to is a manipulator and most possibly a narcissist.

- **Insecure about your achievements:** Since narcissists believe that they are the best thing in the whole universe, it is usually hard, if not borderline impossible, for them to appreciate other people's achievements. Trying to discuss your achievements with a narcissist usually triggers their insecurities - and in fact, make them jealous. Hence, it is usual for a narcissist to try to escape the topic by cutting you off or changing the conversation. Additionally, a narcissist might try to disparage your achievements behind your back by making up lies to discredit you.

Machiavellianism

Machiavellianism is a political philosophy that originated from Niccolò Machiavelli, who lived from 1469 until 1527 in Italy. The political philosophy is of the view that politics is amoral and that any means – however unscrupulous – can justifiably be used in achieving political power.

Machiavelli wrote a political treatise titled The Prince, in which he stated that sincerity, honesty, and other virtues were certainly admirable qualities, but that in politics, the capacity to engage in deceit, treachery, and other forms of criminal behavior was acceptable if there were no other means of achieving political aims to protect one's interests.

However, popular misconceptions have reduced this entire philosophy to the view that "the end justifies the means." Although to be fair, Machiavelli himself insisted that the most important part of this equation lies in ensuring that the end itself must first be justified. However, he added that it is usually better to achieve such ends using means devoid of treachery whenever possible because through this way there is less risk to the interests of the actor.

Therefore, seeking the most effective means of achieving a political end may not necessarily lead to the most treacherous. Besides, not all political ends that have been justified as worth pursuing must be pursued. In many cases, the mere threat that a certain course of action may be pursued may be enough to achieve that end. In some cases, the treachery may be as mild as making a credible threat to take action that is not really even intended.

Thus, in contemporary society, Machiavellianism is a term used to describe people who are perceived as employing Machiavellian tactics to pursue their political agendas.

However, in psychology, the Machiavellianism scale is used to measure the degree to which people with deviant personalities display manipulative behavior. In contemporary society, many people overlook the fact that Machiavellianism is part of the "Dark Triad" of dark psychology and thereby tacitly approve of the deviant behavior of political and business leaders who are able to amass great power or wealth. However, as a psychological disorder, Machiavellianism is entirely different from a chosen path to political power.

The person displaying Machiavellian personality traits does not consider whether his or her actions are the most effective means to achieving his or her goals, whether there are alternatives that do not involve deceit or treachery, or even whether the ultimate result of his or her actions is worth achieving. The Machiavellian personality is not evidence of a strategic or calculating mind attempting to achieve a worthwhile objective in a contentious environment. Instead, it is always on whether the situation calls for a cold, calculating, and manipulative approach or not.

Machiavellians are always on the lookout for themselves. They are deceptive, sly, distrustful as well as manipulative. In fact, Machiavellians see others as a means to their own selfish ends. They tend to be like puppeteers pulling strings that serve to control the actions of others for their own gain.

For instance, it is normal to "call in sick" to work when we really just want a day off. For most people, such conduct is not how they behave normally, and after such an act of dishonesty, they would naturally feel guilty. However, those who display a high degree of Machiavellianism would not just lie when they want a day off; they regard lying and dishonesty as the only way to conduct themselves in all situations, regardless of whether doing so results in any benefit. And they never feel any sort of remorse afterward.

What is more, because of the degree of social acceptance and tacit approval granted to Machiavellian personalities who successfully attain political power, their presence in society does not receive the kind of negative attention accorded to the other two members of the Dark Triad – psychopathy and narcissism.

Basically, traits associated with Machiavellianism include duplicity, manipulation, self-interest, and a lack of both emotion and morality.

Machiavellianism Traits

- **They show signs of duplicity:** Machiavellians are known to be duplicitous in nature. They can be completely different people from one day to the next. It all depends on who they are talking to and what they might be needing from them. In other words, you actually have no idea what their true intentions are because they constantly tell you one thing and do another.

- **Selfishly focused on their own well-being:** Humans are naturally self-interested; hence, it is normal for anyone to focus on their own well-being. You cannot tag someone as a Machiavellian for taking care of themselves. However, there is a point when it goes overboard. People who rank high as Machiavellians believe that in order to get ahead, they must be deceptive. A Machiavellian is only ever going to be concerned with their own well-being. They will not really care about the feelings or the well-being of other people. Hence, they believe in achieving whatever is good for their own well-being at any cost.

- **They dispense information tactically:** They reveal information solely for specific reasons that is usually advantageous to them. They never tell you something just for the sake of you knowing it. Whenever a Machiavellian tells you something, it is usually because they are either fishing for information about you or they want to get something from you.

- **They manipulate and control:** Machiavellians study the people around them. They study and observe your actions until they know what makes you act the way you act. Then they use their knowledge of you to try to manipulate and control you into doing their bidding.

- **They are narcissistic:** Machiavellians are usually narcissistic in nature. Machiavellians are only concerned about themselves. Self-interest is one thing, but they are usually on a whole different level as they think that they are the most important people on earth. Hence, they tend to use you and throw you away if it means they push ahead.

- **They show signs of psychopathic tendencies:** They may be deranged psychopaths who only want to wreak havoc and destruction in the lives of the people around them. And if you see that that is genuinely the case, then you need to act. You have to make sure that you are not putting yourself in this person's path of destruction.

- **They believe that the ends justify the means:** This is probably the most popular philosophical principle that Machiavellians have. This is the type of belief that leads them to act so ruthlessly in their lives. They believe that they are free to do whatever they want so as long as it yields favorable results. They do not care much about the process.

- **They are very toxic to be around:** Machiavellians are just downright toxic. You get the sense that they bring so much negativity and toxicity into your life. You always feel so heavy and overwhelmed whenever you spend time with them.

- **They are very charming:** A lot of these Machiavellians are very charming. They are very good at presenting themselves as people you can trust and rely on. That is why they are able to really charm you and gain your trust as they know the right words to say to get people to trust them.

Psychopathy

Psychopathy is a mental disorder with several identifiable characteristics which include antisocial behavior, amorality, an inability to develop empathy or to establish meaningful personal relationships, extreme egocentricity, and recidivism – with repeated violations resulting from an apparent inability to learn from the consequences of earlier transgressions. Of the three Dark Triad traits, psychopathy is regarded as the most dangerous and insidious of them all – this is because psychopaths are extremely impulsive and they enjoy inflicting harm on others, especially when they do not have their way.

The four major points under psychopathy are antisocial behavior, egocentricity, lack of empathy and amorality.

- Antisocial behavior includes any behavior based upon a goal of violating formal and/or informal rules of social conduct through criminal activity or through acts of personal, private protest, or opposition, all of which is directed against other individuals or society in general.

- Egocentricity is a behavior where the offending person sees himself or herself as the central focus of the world, or at least of all dominant social and political activity.

- Empathy is the ability to view and understand events, thoughts, emotions, and beliefs from the perspective of others, and is considered one of the most important psychological components for establishing successful, ongoing relationships. However, individuals suffering from psychopathy have no iota of empathy; hence the reason why they are able to emotionlessly carry out their acts of psychopathy.

- Amorality should not be confused with immorality as they are entirely different from each other. An immoral act is an act that violates established moral codes. A person who is immoral can be confronted with his or her actions with the expectation that he or she will recognize that his or her actions are offensive from a moral, if not a legal, standpoint. Amorality, on the other hand, represents a psychology deficiency that does not recognize that any moral codes exist, or if they do, that they have no value in determining whether or not to act in one way or another. Hence, someone displaying psychopathy may commit horrendous acts that cause tremendous psychological and physical trauma and not ever understand that what he or she has done is wrong. Even worse, those who display signs of psychopathy usually worsen over time because they are unable to make the connection between the problems in their lives as well as in the lives of those around them and their own harmful and destructive actions.

Basically, personality traits associated with psychopathy include a lack of empathy or remorse, antisocial behavior, and being manipulative and volatile in nature.

Common Signs of Psychopathy

Listed below are few common signs of psychopathy you need to be aware of; they include:

- Socially irresponsible behavior
- Disregarding or violating the rights of others
- Inability to distinguish between right and wrong
- Difficulty with showing remorse or empathy

- A tendency to lie often
- Manipulating and hurting others
- Recurring problems with the law
- General disregard towards safety and responsibility

Other behaviors that may be signs of psychopathy include a tendency to take excessive risks, reckless behavior, and being deceitful with frequent lying.

Identifying Dark Triad Traits

Now that you know the three personality traits that define dark psychology, I bet you must be wondering if there is a way to easily identify if a friend, family member, or even yourself possess any of the Dark Triad traits.

There are a number of ways you can use to identify Dark Triad traits, but most of them are fairly complicated. However, there is a fairly straightforward "test" that was developed in 2010 by Dr. Peter Jonason and Gregory Webster. This "test" is referred to as the "Dirty Dozen" rating scale and it can be used to measure Dark Triad traits in any individual.

The Dirty Dozen rating scale includes twelve statements that you need to rate yourself to on a scale of one to seven. The higher the score, the higher the probability of the person possessing Dark Triad tendencies. The statements are as follows:

1. I tend to manipulate others to get my way.
2. I have used deceit or lied to get my way.
3. I tend to lack remorse.
4. I tend to seek prestige or status.
5. I tend to expect special favors from others
6. I tend to not be too concerned with morality or the morality of my actions.
7. I tend to be callous or insensitive.
8. I tend to be cynical.
9. I tend to want others to admire me.
10. I tend to want others to pay attention to me.
11. I have used flattery to get my way.
12. I tend to exploit others towards my own end.

To easily identify if a friend, family member, or even yourself possess Dark Triad tendencies, simply answer the questions above as honestly as you can or ask your friends or family to answer the questions as honestly as they can.

Managing People with Dark Triad Traits

If after taking the test above, you discover that a friend, a family member, or even a colleague at work possesses Dark Triad traits, I believe the next step is learning how to manage them. However, before we get to that, there are three major ways through which people can exhibit their Dark Triad traits; they are:

- Through psychopathic anger
- Through manipulation
- Through narcissism

In the subsequent paragraphs, I will be discussing how you can manage people that exhibit these traits. However, before I proceed, you should keep in mind that there is no easy and straightforward way to manage people with Dark Triad traits. This is because everyone has a different personality type and as you might know, the behaviors associated with these personality types tend to change on a daily basis. Hence, try to put this into consideration while you are trying to manage people with Dark Triad traits.

Managing Psychopathic Anger

People with psychopathic traits are prone to anger and aggression. If you tend to spend time around such people, you must learn to defuse angry and aggressive situations as speedily as you can. Usually, the signs of normal anger are not hard to spot. These signs include:

- Sweating, especially in the palms and armpits
- Visibly shaking or trembling
- Flushed face
- Clenching of jaws and/or grinding of teeth
- Raised voice

However, some people tend to suppress their anger, which then ends up showing itself in passive-aggressive ways such as:

- Displaying a cynical, sullen, or hostile attitude
- Sulking around or acting stubborn

- Intentionally making mistakes so as to get a reaction out of you

Dealing with angry people can be extremely exhausting; however, there are a number of strategies you can employ when dealing with such people. They include the following:

- **Safety first then external intervention:** If you ever feel that a person is getting too angry to the point that they might try to hurt you, trust your instinct and do you best to leave the vicinity. Do not make the mistake of trying to appease an extremely angry person; sometimes, during the heat of anger, appeasement tends to make a psychotic individual more pissed. However, often times than not, when they have no one or nothing to direct their anger at, they tend to calm down.

After leaving, you can then get someone to intervene in the matter. Oftentimes, the presence of another individual will prevent the angry individual from doing anything drastic.

- **Try to identify the cause of their anger:** After seeking safety and when the situation has calmed down a bit, you can then try to determine why the person you are dealing with feels angry. To achieve this, you need to use effective questioning techniques to get to the root of their anger. Encourage them to explain why they feel angry. Do you best not to interrupt them while they speak – as this can lead to an argument that can set them off again. Keep asking them questions until they fully explain why they were angry. After they have explained the cause of their anger, and it is your turn to speak, speak slowly and calmly, and try not to use a threatening body language. All these will encourage them to calm down.

- **Never respond with anger:** Of course, it is very natural to get upset when angry people confront you. However, responding with anger is the quickest way to escalate an already volatile situation. Whenever someone confronts you angrily, do your best to respond as calmly as you can. It is easier said than done, but you can achieve this by learning how to manage your emotions so that you can stay relaxed during tense situations. One of the ways to manage your emotions and prevent yourself from getting upset is by practicing deep breathing – this will help you regulate your heartbeat and gradually dispel any negative energy from your system.

- **Do not take every angry situation personally:** Sometimes, a person's anger has nothing to do with you – especially when you are confident that you did nothing wrong. For instance, a person might be angry because they received some bad news and taking out their anger at the bad news on you might be making them feel better. Recognizing that you are not the cause of the anger can help you not take their angry outbursts personally. Hence, when someone suddenly starts showing signs of anger either through the normal ways or through the passive-aggressive way, it is important that you try to determine if you are the cause of their anger. If you are not, you can try your best to ignore their angry antics and not take it personally. On the other hand, if you find out that you are responsible for their anger, you still have no reason to take it personally. Simply apologize and try not to repeat what made them angry.

- **Distract them:** Besides the above-mentioned strategies, one way to manage a person's anger and potentially defuse it is to try and distract them from their anger. You can do this by focusing their anger on something else. Basically, whenever a person keeps ruminating on their anger, they tend to get angrier. By distracting them you are taking their mind off their anger and focusing it on something else – the less they have cause to think about their anger, the less they get angry.

Managing Manipulators

Machiavellians are very good manipulators. They tend to manipulate people by selfishly influencing them through coercion and/or deception. Additionally, they are often good at hiding their manipulative behaviors and actions under the guise of innocence. Regardless of this, there are a couple of signs you can look out for when you feel that a person is exhibiting manipulative tendencies. These signs include the following:

- A person that never takes "no" for an answer.
- Someone who always tries to excuse their hurtful behavior.
- Someone who usually presents a different personality to different people in order to serve their selfish purposes.
- A person that is always trying to get you to do what they want at all times.

You can manage people with manipulative tendencies with the following strategies:

- **Challenge them:** Manipulative people tend to get away with their acts of manipulation because most people would rather not confront them. However, this is counterintuitive because lack of confrontation makes manipulative people bolder with their manipulative acts. Hence, one of the ways through which you can manage manipulative people is to challenge them whenever you notice their manipulative acts. When challenging them, you need to be specific about the manipulative actions you have spotted and let them know how those actions are affecting you. Often times than not, after challenging a manipulator, they tend to leave you alone because they realize that you are not an easy meat – so to speak.

- **Learn to stand your ground:** Sometimes, challenging a manipulator can make them more determined to come after you. This is when you stand your ground and let such a person know that you would not stand for any nonsense. You must make it clear to such a person that they must change their behavior towards you. Let them know that you plan to hold them accountable if they do not.

- **Avoid them whenever you can:** If the aforementioned tactics fail, your only resort might be to avoid them at all costs. It will be difficult for them to try to manipulate you if they do not have access to you. Hence, do your best to stay away from them whenever you can.

Managing Narcissism

Narcissists have a slew of underhand tactics which they employ manipulating their partners as well as the people around them. The ultimate aim of a narcissist is to destroy their partner's reality and confidence so as to gain or keep control over the relationship and their partner's lives. To do this, a narcissist would use any form of abuse such as emotional abuse, mental abuse, physical abuse, financial abuse, spiritual abuse, as well as sexual abuse. Their modus operandi is to set a person up to feel crazy, thereby making it less likely for them to reach out to their family and friends for help because they feel that no one will believe them.

Here are a couple examples of abuse commonly used by narcissists:

- **Being verbally abusive:** Verbal abuse includes belittling, accusing, blaming, bullying, criticizing, shaming, and threatening you. Although verbal abuse alone does not mean that you are dealing with a narcissist, when used together with other forms of abuse it tends to be narcissistic in nature.

- **Emotional blackmail:** Another form of manipulation narcissist tends to make use of is emotional blackmail. They can blackmail you emotionally by making you feel fear, guilt, or doubt. Likewise, they may use anger, intimidation, threats, warnings, or punishment as means of keeping you in line.

- **Manipulation:** Narcissists tend to manipulate people by skillfully using words or actions to get what they want from a person. They do this by preying on your fears, sense of guilt, or sense of obligation with the sole aim of getting their needs fulfilled.

- **Gaslighting:** Narcissists tend to use gaslighting as a means of making you distrust your views of reality or believe that you are mentally unstable. As a matter of fact, gaslighting is one of the favorite tools of a narcissist.

- **Negative comparison:** Unnecessarily making comparisons to negatively contrast you with themself or other people is another form of abuse that narcissists like to use.

- **Persistently lying:** Narcissists persistently use deception to avoid responsibility or to achieve their own ends. Hence, if a person is constantly lying to you and trying to deceive you, they are most definitely abusing you psychologically.

- **Withholding:** A narcissist might also abuse you by withholding things such as money, sex, communication, or affection from you as a means of keeping you in line or as a means of trying to get you to do their bidding.

- **Character assassination:** Another form of abuse that narcissists like to make use of is character assassination which involves spreading malicious gossip or lies about you to other people.

- **Playing the victim card:** When all else fails, the narcissist resorts to playing the victim card. This is a form of emotional manipulation that is designed to gain your sympathy and further control your behavior.

As you can see from the list above, narcissists are highly selfish and inconsiderate. However, since the ultimate aim of a narcissist is to deflate your morale, their selfishness tends to be a major source of headache rather than a source of threat. In fact, due to their selfish nature, narcissists may not even realize the impact of their actions, hence, it is important to call their attention to any narcissistic act the moment you notice it. Make sure to stand your ground and meet their claims or demands with solid counter-arguments as this is the only way you can truly get them to change their behavior towards you.

Chapter 3: Dark Psychology Manipulation Techniques

There are numerous dark psychology manipulation techniques; however, in this book, I will be discussing the four major dark psychological techniques that most people employ. Needless to say, learning about these nefarious techniques can help you easily identify them in people around you. Also, learning about these techniques is the first step to learning how to protect yourself against such. You would agree with me that you cannot protect yourself against something you have no knowledge about. So, let us get to it.

Gaslighting

The concept of gaslighting originated from an old movie titled "Gaslit". The movie shows a man trying to manipulate his wife into making her think that she is losing her sense of reality so that he can send her to a mental institution and take over her inheritance. While not all cases of gaslighting are that drastic, the ultimate aim of any gaslighter is to make their victim lose touch with reality.

Gaslighting is perhaps the cruelest form of dark psychological manipulation. It involves casting into doubt the sanity and self-esteem of a person. You could say it is like sowing the seeds of doubt into the victim of the manipulation. Gaslighting works on the principle of "knowing you are being told repeated lies" until you eventually begin to believe such lies as the truth. Needless to say, it is an unkind form of manipulation.

Usually, the gaslighter causes their victim to lose all confidence in their own credibility by systematically destroying their self-worth until they begin to doubt themselves. The ultimate intention of gaslighting is to reduce the victim to a psychological mess. The manipulator will constantly put their target down by contradicting them and by convincing them that they are always wrong; sometimes to the point that the victim will be accused of telling lies. As a result of these, the victim slowly loses all self-esteem until they begin to believe the lies the gaslighter tells them. When this happens, the victim then becomes ruled and controlled by the domineering influencer.

Gaslighting, whether intentional or not, is a form of manipulation. Gaslighting can happen in many types of relationships, including those with bosses, friends, and parents. But one of the most devastating forms of gaslighting is when it occurs in a relationship between a couple.

Gaslighting is a form of mental abuse that is often seen in abusive personal relationships. The influencer/gaslighter will constantly use different techniques with the ultimate intention to make their victim doubt themselves. The moment the victim gives in to doubt, it is over. The gaslighter has won.

How Gaslighting Happens

A gaslighter can employ numerous techniques intended to manipulate you, they include:

- **Countering:** A gaslighter uses the countering technique to sow the seed of doubt into their victim's mind. For instance, their victim might be talking about a particular memory that they shared with the gaslighter, the gaslighter would then counter the memory with their own version and insist that their own version is the correct version. This technique is another way gaslighter cast doubts into the minds of their victims. If it is done frequently, it would get to a point where the victim would start doubting and questioning their own memories.

- **Withholding**: One of the tactics employed by is withholding information from their victim. They might refuse to engage in a conversation or they may pretend not to understand what you are saying so that they would not have to respond to you. Ultimately, a gaslighter uses this technique to escape being accountable for their gaslighting actions as well as to further plunge their victim into confusion.

- **Diversion:** A gaslighter uses this technique whenever their victim tries to talk to them about their gaslighting actions. Instead of engaging in a conversation, the gaslighter would systematically divert their victim's attention from the issue at hand. They might do this by making a comment completely unrelated to what their victim is talking about.

- **Trivializing:** This is a favorite technique of a gaslighter. This technique involves the gaslighter disregarding or belittling the feelings of their victims. They do this by making their victim feel that their feelings or thoughts are unimportant. Regardless of how valid their victim's concerns are, they might go further to accuse them of overreacting to things or being overly sensitive.

- **Denial:** Another favorite technique of a gaslighter. A gaslighter uses the denial technique to by pretending to forget certain events and how they occurred. Under this technique, it is common for a gaslighter to deny something they previously said and accuse you of making things up. The ultimate aim of this technique, just like the others, is to gradually condition their victim to believe that they cannot rely on their memories.

Gaslighting and Narcissism

It is common for gaslighters to have the psychological disorder known as Narcissistic Personality Disorder. In fact, out of the three Dark Triad traits, narcissists are usually the ones that utilize gaslighting as a manipulation technique. This is because they are attracted to the insidious nature of gaslighting – when gaslighting is done perfectly, the victims might not realize that they are being gaslighted.

As I mentioned earlier, narcissists always tend to be self-absorbed and as a result, they usually have no interest in other people unless it serves a purpose for them. Due to their lack of empathy, they are usually unable to understand what their victims are feeling – to them, it is just all a big game.

A person with a narcissistic personality disorder may:

- Project an inflated sense of self-importance
- Exaggerate their achievements
- Respond to criticism with anger
- Use others for personal gain
- Expect special consideration or special treatment
- Be highly critical of others
- Become envious and jealous easily

The ultimate aim of a narcissistic gaslighter is to gain absolute control over their victims. Hence, their first step is to break down their victims through gaslighting techniques. The narcissist does this until their victim begins to doubt or question their own perspectives and reality, until they start difficulty trusting themselves, their sanity, and even their reality. All of this coalesces to a point where their victims develop low self-esteem and start exhibiting dependency tendencies. The aim of the narcissistic manipulator is accomplished when these things happen and from that point onward, they can start imposing their wishes on their broken victim without encountering much resistance.

Brainwashing

Brainwashing refers to a method of thought reform through social influence. This kind of social influence happens throughout the day to every single one of us, whether we realize it or not. For instance, compliance regulations that are adopted in the workplace are, in one way or the other, a form of brainwashing as they require you to think and act in a specific way whenever you are on the job.

In terms of dark psychology, brainwashing refers to the process whereby a person or a group of people make use of some underhand methods to talk someone into changing their will to that of the manipulator. When discussing the concept of brainwashing, it is important to differentiate between honest persuasion and brainwashing, as there are several ways that people persuade one another these days, especially in the field of politics.

Basically, persuasion seeks to influence the behaviors, motivations, intentions, attitudes, and beliefs of the subject. One of the ways that people persuade others to conform to their will is by stating a few things that could typically induce a "yes" response from the target. They then use some statements of facts as the icing on the cake. In the end, they state what it is that they want people to do. As an example, consider this statement: "Are you tired of paying exorbitant fares for your child's schooling? What about the rising prices of gas and power supply? Are you concerned about the constant riots and strikes? Well, a good point to recall is that the incumbent government has mentioned that the country is gradually drawing close to recession and that the prices of fuel will continue to rise as they are seeing the greatest drop in the economy since the end of the civil war. However, we – democrats – believe otherwise! Therefore, if you want the country to change for the better, make sure you go out and vote for democrats." The aforementioned statement is not necessarily a brainwashing attempt and can be regarded as an attempt to persuade the people to vote for a particular political party.

Brainwashing, on the other hand, involves convincing someone to abandon their past beliefs in order to adopt new values and ideals. Brainwashing can be done in a lot of ways; however, not of those ways are intrinsically bad. For example, an African person that chooses to migrate to Europe will inevitably be forced to change their values and ideals so as to fit in to the new culture and traditions of the European country they move to. Needless to say, that cannot be regarded as an outright form of brainwashing. On the other hand, an instance of outright brainwashing can be seen from how those in concentration camps or in countries where a new dictator government is taking over will be treated. These people often will have to go through a process of brainwashing in order for them to be "convinced" to follow along peacefully.

With all these being said, in order for brainwashing to work effectively, the subject or target will need to go through the brainwashing process under complete isolation due to the invasive influence on the subject. This is one of the reasons that a lot of brainwashing cases that you might have heard about tend to occur in totalistic cults or prison camps.

For a brainwashing process to be successful, the brainwasher must be able to gain total control over their subject. This means that they must be able to control the fulfillment of every basic human needs of the victim such as their sleeping patterns and eating habits. During this brainwashing process, the brainwasher will work to systematically break down the subject's whole identity, and once the identity is broken, the brainwasher will then proceed to replace it with the desired beliefs, attitudes, and behaviors.

Steps Used in Brainwashing

The brainwashing steps I will be discussing in this book was developed by a psychologist known as Robert Jay Lifton. After studying former prisoners of the Korean War as well as prisoners from Chinese war camps, Robert came up with ten steps that were used in the brainwashing process of these prisoners. These steps are:

1. Assault on identity
2. Guilt
3. Self-betrayal
4. Breaking point
5. Leniency
6. Compulsion to confess
7. Channeling of guilt
8. Releasing of guilt
9. Progress and harmony
10. Final confession and rebirth

As I mentioned earlier, for any brainwashing process to be successful, it has to take place in an environment that is totally isolated from the outside world. Although Robert broke down the process into ten steps, I will organize those steps into three broad stages so that you can better understand what a subject basically goes through during a brainwashing process.

Let us take a look at those three stages:

Breaking down the victim's identity

The first stage of the brainwashing process involves breaking down the old identity of the victim. This is done to make the victim feel vulnerable and open to the new identity the brainwasher wants to force on them.

The step is very important as well as instrumental to the success of the brainwashing technique. If the brainwasher fails to completely break down the victim's identity, it will be difficult – if not borderline impossible – for them to make the victim adopt another identity. Hence, breaking down the victim's identity, up to the point that they start to question their previous beliefs, makes it easier for the victim to adopt a new identity later on in the brainwashing process.

Breaking down the victim's identity can be done in the following steps discussed below:

- **Assault the victim's identity:** This step basically revolves around getting the subject to believe that they are not who they think they are. This step involves a systematic attack on everything that makes up a victim's identity such as their core beliefs. Under this step, the brainwasher tries to make the victim believe that they are not what they are. For instance, if the victim was previously a Christian, the brainwasher will constantly attack them for days, weeks, months trying to make them believe that they are not a Christian. This attack goes on until the victim becomes mentally disoriented and starts to doubt if they were previously a Christian.

- **Guilting the victim:** This step basically revolves around guilting the subject into feeling that they are bad or that there is something wrong with them. This step invokes a deep sense of guilt in the victim, making them feel that their badness or wrongness needs to be fixed. While the victim is experiencing an identity crisis from the first step, the brainwasher will simultaneously create an overwhelming sense of guilt in the target. They will repeatedly and mercilessly attack the subject for any "sin" the target has committed. They will criticize the victim for everything, from the "evilness" of their beliefs to the way they eat slowly or quickly, until the target begins to feel a general sense of shame, that everything they do is, in one way or the other, wrong, or bad.

- **Forcing the victim to self-betrayal:** This step basically revolves around forcing the victim into agreeing that they are bad. As soon as the victim becomes disoriented from the assault on their identity and while they are feeling a deep sense of guilt, the brainwasher then forces the victim to denounce everything associated with their previous identity. This usually involves forcing the victim to forsake their friends and family that share the same "wrong" belief that the victim previously subscribed to. Betraying their own beliefs as well as forsaking those people they feel a sense of loyalty to ultimately increases the shame and loss of identity of the victim. Sometimes, this self-betrayal is too great for the victim to handle and this pushes them to a breaking point.

- **Pushing the victim to their breaking point:** With the identity of the subject in crisis while experiencing a deep sense of shame for having betrayed what they had always believed in, the victim may undergo what is referred to as a "nervous breakdown." This breakdown may involve uncontrollable sobbing, deep depression, and general disorientation. The victim may lose their grip on reality and have the feeling of being completely lost and alone. When the victim reaches their breaking point, their sense of self is pretty much up for grabs as they have no clear understanding of who they are or what is happening to them. At this point, the brainwasher then sets up the temptation to convert them to another belief system. The brainwasher will project this as something that will save the victim from their misery.

The Possibility of Salvation

After successfully breaking down the victim's identity, which ultimately results in the victim having a nervous breakdown, the brainwasher then moves to the next stage. This next stage involves offering the victim the possibility of salvation after they have had a nervous breakdown. The brainwasher lets the victim know that they can feel better if only they are willing to turn away from their former belief system and embrace the new one that is being offered.

The "possibility of salvation" stage is usually carried out through the four steps listed below:

- **Offering leniency:** After the victim has undergone constant abuse to the point that they have finally broken down, the brainwasher offers some leniency in form of a small kindness or reprieve from the constant abuse – this small kindness can be in the form of offering the victim some clean water or even asking about what they miss about their old life. After undergoing constant psychological attack, this act of kindness seems overly magnanimous and it makes the victim experience a sense of relief and gratitude that is completely disproportionate to the little act of kindness. In fact, at this stage, it is common for such little act of kindness to make the victim feel as if the brainwasher just saved their life or something.

- **Confession:** The disproportional relief the victim fees from the little act of leniency then inspires a desire in them to want to reciprocate the kindness offered to them. At this point, the brainwasher then presents the victim with the possibility of confessing the "sins" of their previous identity. The brainwasher lets the victim know that this act of confession will relieve them of any guilt and pain they might be feeling.

- **Channeling of guilt:** After weeks or months of assault, confusion, breakdown, and moments of leniency, the victim's guilt have lost all meaning – he or she is not sure what they have done wrong, they just know that they are wrong. This creates something of a blank slate that lets the brainwasher fill in the blanks. The brainwasher then attaches that guilt, that sense of "wrongness," to whatever he or she wants; usually, the victim's guilt is attached to the belief system the brainwasher is trying to replace. The victim then comes to believe it is his or her belief system that caused his or her shame. Thus, the contrast between old and new has been established; the old belief system is associated with psychological (and usually physical) agony while the new belief system is associated with the possibility of escaping that agony.

- **Releasing of guilt:** At this point, the victim is now relieved to learn there that there is an external cause for their wrongness or badness, that it is not that they are inexorably bad. This means they can escape the wrongness by denouncing and abandoning the wrong belief system. The victim now believes that all they have to do is to denounce everything associated with their previous belief system and pain will end. The victim now feels that they have the power to release themselves from the wrongness by confessing to acts associated with their old belief system. With their full confessions, the victim has completed the psychological rejection of their former identity. It is now up to the brainwasher to offer the victim a new identity.

Rebuilding the victim's identity

This is the third and final stage in the brainwashing process. By this stage, the victim has undergone a series of ordeals meant to strip them of their old identity. At this stage, the victim has realized that their previous belief system was the cause of the wrongness they were feeling and that they need to change it in order to feel normal again. Hence, the brainwasher now starts rebuilding the identity of the victim by implanting the ideals and values of the new system into the mind of the victim. At this point, the victim is a clean slate and is very eager to learn the new system that would make them feel better.

Rebuilding the victim's identity is done through the two steps listed below:

- **Progress and harmony:** Under this step, the brainwasher introduces a new belief system as the path to becoming "good." At this stage, the brainwasher would have stopped the abuse, offering the victim physical comfort and mental calm in concurrence with the new belief system. The victim is made to feel that it is they who must choose between old and new, thereby giving the victim the sense that their fate is in their own hands. Since the victim has already denounced their old belief system in response to leniency and torment and has made a "conscious choice" in favor of the contrasting belief system, this helps to further relieve his guilt. Therefore, the choice is not a difficult one because by now, the subject believes that the new identity is safe and desirable. After all, it is nothing like the one that led to their previous breakdown.

- **Final confession and rebirth:** By comparing the agony of the old belief system with the peacefulness of the new belief system, the victim then chooses the new identity, clinging to it like a life preserver. The victim rejects the old belief system and pledges allegiance to the new belief system – which they believe will make their life better. Usually, at this final stage, there are often ceremonies used to welcome the converted victim to their new community. The newly transformed victim is then allowed to embrace their new identity and is welcomed with open arms into the new community. Instead of being isolated and alone, the victim now has many new friends and community members on their side. Instead of feeling the guilt and pain that has plagued the subject for many months, the victim now feels happiness and peacefulness. The new identity is now the victims' and the brainwashing transformation is thereby complete. The victim has been successfully rebirthed with a new identity and belief system.

As you may have gleaned, the process of brainwashing can take place over a period of many months or even years. Naturally, most people are set in their identity and the beliefs that they have; hence, it is not possible to change all of this in just a few days unless the person was already willing to change – and that would make the brainwashing techniques unnecessary. Also, isolation would be necessary because outside influences will prevent the subject from relying on the brainwasher during this process, and this is why most of the brainwashing cases occur in prison camps and other isolated places.

Hence, you do not need to be alarmed at being brainwashed. The fact that you are surrounded with people as well as technology will render the brainwashing process useless against you. Only a person in isolation can be successfully brainwashed, and even at that, the process generally takes a long time due to the numerous steps needed to change the identity and belief system of an individual.

Hypnosis

Hypnosis is a dark manipulation technique that most people have little or no knowledge about. In fact, if you ask most people what they know about manipulation, they will probably narrate stage acts where the hypnotist tries to hypnotize their volunteers into doing something they would not do on a good day. Although that is a form of hypnosis, it is a minuscule part of the concept of hypnosis.

Hypnosis is a trancelike state that resembles sleep but is induced by a person whose suggestions are willingly accepted by the subject. When a person is hypnotized, they basically enter a different state of mind in which they will be susceptible to obeying the suggestions provided by the hypnotist.

However, before a person is hypnotized, they have to successfully undergo three stages, which are: induction, suggestion, and susceptibility. Just like the stages under the brainwashing process, each of the aforementioned stages are important to the success of a person being hypnotized.

Let us take a look at these stages of hypnosis and how they are carried out.

Susceptibility

Before an individual can be hypnotized, the hypnotist has to make sure that such individual will be susceptible to the process of hypnosis. People tend to respond differently to the process of hypnosis; some people can easily fall into a hypnotic trance while it takes a lot of time and effort before other people become hypnotized. Hence, it is left to the hypnotist to determine if their target is susceptible to the influences of hypnotism. One of the ways a hypnotist usually tries to find out the susceptibility of their target is by conducting an eye-roll test. The target is asked to roll their eyes upward, then the hypnotist observes if he can still see the iris and cornea of the target's eye. Basically, the less the iris and cornea are seen, the more susceptible a person is to being hypnotized. Conversely, the more the iris and cornea are seen, the less susceptible a person is to being hypnotized.

Induction

After determining the level of susceptibility in their target, if a hypnotist finds out that their target is highly susceptible to being hypnotized, they then begin the process of induction.

The induction stage is where the hypnotist will prime the subject on all the steps needed to lead the participant in the desired direction of being hypnotized. There are several induction processes a hypnotist can try; however, I will be describing the most popular induction process known as Braidism.

To use the Braidism technique, the hypnotist will have to follow a couple of steps highlighted below:

- The first step requires taking an object – preferably a bright object such as a metallic stopwatch. Then the hypnotist will hold this object in front of the subject, keeping the object about 8-15 inches from the subject's eyes.

- Next, the hypnotist will inform their subject to ensure that their eyes are always fixed on the object. The hypnotist will also inform the subject to completely focus their attention on the object. In fact, for the induction process to work, the subject must not think about any other thing except the object.

- After a short time of focusing on the object, the subject's eyes will begin to dilate. To know if the subject is truly under a trance, the hypnotist will then move their fingers from the subject's eyes to the object. After completing this motion, if the subject closes their eyes involuntarily, they are in a trance. If this does not happen, then the process will have to be started all over again until the subject transitions into an altered state of mind.

Suggestion

After successfully inducting the subject into an altered state of mind, the hypnotist then has full rein on manipulating the subject into doing their bidding. They do this by "suggesting" what they want the victim to do. Their suggestion can be delivered as direct verbal suggestions that include using insinuations, metaphors, and figures of speech. However, on some occasions, their suggestion might be in a non-verbal form such as using physical manipulation, voice tonality, and mental imagery to get their victims to do their bidding.

Emotional Blackmail

Emotional blackmail is a style of dark manipulation whereby someone uses your feelings as a way to control your behavior or persuade you to see things their way. With this technique, the manipulator will seek to inspire sympathy or guilt in their subject. These are the two strongest emotions that humans feel and they are often enough to spur the subject into doing what the manipulator wants. The manipulator usually takes advantage of this fact in order to get what they want; they will use the sympathy or the guilt that they stimulate to coerce the subject into cooperating or helping them. Usually, the degree of sympathy or guilt will be blown out of proportion, thereby making the subject even more likely to help out in the situation.

The point of using emotional blackmail is to play on the emotions of the subject so that they might feel as if they are helping out of their own free will. With regular blackmail, the subject has a threat to deal with, mostly in terms of physical harm to themselves or someone they love. However, with emotional blackmail, the manipulator will work to arouse emotions that are strong enough to spur the subject to action. These emotions may make the subject think that they are helping out of their own free will, while in reality, the manipulator is the one pushing the buttons.

Understanding the dynamics of emotional manipulation will be useful in helping you extricate yourself from the controlling behavior of another person or to deal with your compulsion to do things that are uncomfortable, undesirable, burdensome, or self-sacrificing for others.

How Emotional Blackmail Works

Emotional blackmail progresses through six specific stages; which are:

Demand: The first stage of emotional blackmail involves a demand. An emotional manipulator may make a demand stating that you should not hang out with a certain person.

They may make this demand outrightly by telling you verbally to "Stay away from that person or else…" or their demand may be made in a more subtle form. For instance, when they see you with the person they told you to stay away from, they might pout or scrunch up their face. This makes you ask them what is wrong, to which they respond, "I don't like how they look at you" or "I don't think they're good for you."

Sure, they dress up their demand in terms of caring about you, but it is still an attempt to control your choice of friend.

Resistance: The second stage of emotional blackmail usually involves you resisting the attempt to be manipulated. From the demand above, you might disagree and tell your other friend that you have the right to hang out with whoever you want. This stage basically involves you thinking that they would drop the demand or forget about it. However, as you would discover in the next stage, they will not give up or forget about it.

Pressure: After resisting their demands, an emotional manipulator might resort to pressuring you into giving in to their demands. Usually, in a normal relationship, once you express resistance to a particular demand your partner is asking from you, they will either drop such demand or try to reach a compromise on the issue. However, reverse is the case with an emotional blackmailer, instead of dropping the demand or looking for ways to reach a compromise, they will rather resort to pressuring you to give in to their demands. They might try repeating their demand in a way that makes them look good (e.g., "I'm only trying to look out for you). Or they might start listing ways your resistance is "negatively" affecting them (e.g., I have been unable to sleep because I keep thinking about why you are resisting my idea).

Emotional blackmailers are usually not concerned about pushing too hard; hence, they will persist until they eventually get what they want.

Threats: If pressurizing you fails to work; an emotional blackmailer will usually resort to threatening you. Their threats might be direct (e.g., if you hang out with that person again, I will break up with you) or indirect (e.g., if you cannot listen to me, maybe you do not deserve me). An emotional manipulator usually makes use of threats as a last resort. They use threats to make you choose between continued resistance or giving in to their demands.

Compliance: Of course, since you do not want them to make good on their threats, you give up and give in. At this stage, you might even wonder if their "request" warranted your resistance in the first instance.

Compliance can be an eventual process, as they wear you down over time with pressure and threats. However, once you give in, the turmoil then gives way to peace. They have gotten what they want, so they might seem particularly kind and loving — at least for the moment.

Repetition: Since you have shown the emotional manipulator that you will eventually concede to their demands, they now know exactly how to play similar situations in the future.

Therefore, over time, the process of emotional blackmail teaches you that it is easier to comply than to face persistent pressure and threats. You may come to accept that their love is conditional and something they will withhold until you agree with them or give in to their demands.

The emotional manipulator might even learn that a particular kind of threat will get the job done faster; hence, as a result, this pattern or cycle or process will probably continue.

Emotional Blackmail Strategies

Typically, there are three strategies emotional manipulators tend to employ; they include fear, obligation, and guilt. An emotional manipulator can use all of these three strategies together or rely on just one or two of them.

Fear: Emotional manipulators are experts at playing on their victim's fear to achieve what they want. Since emotional blackmail usually occurs in close relationships, the blackmailer leverages their knowledge of the victim's fears. They use the fears of the victim to manipulate them into doing what they want.

An emotional manipulator can utilize different types of fears such as fear of abandonment, fear of confrontation, fear of tricky situations, and fear for physical safety to make their victim comply with their requests. No one wants to be in a position of fear and emotional manipulators know this and will usually exploit this weakness in their victims. A lot of people will do anything not to feel fearful, and since the fear is coming from the emotional manipulator who wants something, the victim inevitably gives in to the manipulator's demand.

Obligation: It is no secret that we tend to feel a sense of obligation to those around us. We feel a sense of loyalty and duty to those people in our lives and this usually makes us do the bidding of those people close to us. Emotional manipulators know this and use every opportunity to remind us of those obligations, pushing the buttons that make us feel duty-bound to do whatever they want. For instance, a parent may remind their child of all the "sacrifices" they made for such child, thereby insinuating that the child is obligated to carry out their wishes.

Guilt: Guilt is very much linked to obligation. If a person does not do something they think they have to do, they tend to experience guilt. Emotional manipulators know this and tend to exploit this. They can guilt-trip their victims for not giving in to their demands, regardless of if the demand is reasonable or not.

Types of Emotional Blackmailing

There are four different types of emotional blackmail and each of these types are executed with various manipulation tactics. You should keep in mind that an emotional blackmailer may adopt one or more of these roles in order to get you to do what they want.

The Punisher: Punishers operate with the need to get their way at all cost. They make demands and expect them to be met, regardless of the feelings and needs of the other person.

Punishers insist on getting whatever they want with threats of punishment if they do not get whatever they are after. The favorite strategy this kind of blackmailer uses the most is fear. They might exploit the victim's fear of being alone by threatening to end the relationship if they fail to give in to their demands.

The Self-punisher: On the other hand, self-punishers threaten to harm themselves if their partner fails to comply with what they need. Basically, self-punishers employ the tactic of punishing or threatening to punish themselves, knowing that it will distress their partner and ultimately force them to do their bidding.

The Sufferer: Sufferers tend to hold their misery over their partner's head as a way of getting them to do what they want. They usually claim that they will suffer if their partner fails to comply with their wishes. Hence, they tend to convey the guilt of their "suffering" to their partner when they fail to comply with their wishes.

The Tantalizer: A tantalizer tends to promise some kind of reward if their wishes are carried out. They manipulate people around them by offering some sort of reward. A tantalizer can go as far as offering sex as a reward if their wishes are attended to. Hence, the promise of a reward usually pushes their victims to comply with their demands.

Categories of Emotionally Manipulative Behavior

Understanding the basic dynamics of manipulative and abusive relationships is important. Psychologists have identified many specific techniques of behavior modification commonly employed by emotional manipulators. Some of these techniques include:

Positive reinforcement: This technique was identified by the behavioral psychologist B.F. Skinner, whose theory of operant conditioning resulted from his experiments with small animals placed in cages. In his experiment to prove the theory of positive reinforcement, he used cages equipped with two levers; one lever did nothing, while the other produced a food pellet whenever the small animal pushed it. Soon, the animals learned through positive reinforcement which lever to push to get their reward.

Emotional manipulators employ positive reinforcement in their strategies by using techniques such as praise, false and superficial demonstrations of emotions such as charm and sympathy, excessive rewards including gifts, money, approval, and attention, and other outward demonstrations of emotion meant to make the victim feel good.

Negative reinforcement: The other part of Skinner's experiment proved the effectiveness of negative reinforcement. For this part of his experiment, small animals were again placed in cages, which were again equipped with two levers. This time, the cages were charged with a mild voltage of electricity that caused slight discomfort to the animals that were placed in them. Once inside the cages, the animals would press one of the two levers. One of the levers did not produce any results, while the other stopped the electrical current, relieving the discomfort. Soon, the animals learned to press the lever that lessened their pain.

Intermittent reinforcement: Intermittent reinforcement can be either positive or negative and is used to create doubt, fear, or uncertainty. An emotional manipulator may "train" his or her victim by imposing inconsistent reward and punishment mechanisms to lessen the victim's sense of confidence, control, and autonomy.

For example, in a romantic relationship, the predator may condition the victim to wear certain clothing, listen to certain music, eat certain types of food, and work at a certain type of job. As the victim in this relationship gains confidence, the predator may begin to discourage their victim, who will be caught off guard. As the victim scrambles to respond, the manipulator may again change tactics.

Punishment: Punishment is a very basic form of emotional manipulation that may involve an entire range of psychologically and emotionally negative and damaging behavior, such as threats, yelling, nagging, complaining, intimidation, insults, guilt, and other forms of emotional blackmail. Skilled predators may find a way to incorporate this abusive and controlling behavior into the relationship over time so that the victim will develop a tolerance for abuse.

Traumatic one-trial learning: This technique is related to the use of punishments, but rather than a feature of a long-term relationship, these techniques involve discrete episodes in which the manipulator uses verbal abuse, demonstrations of anger, and other forms of dominance and intimidation to discourage the victim from certain types of behavior.

Chapter 4: The Effects of Dark Psychological Abuse

The effects of dark psychological abuse are experienced by both the perpetrator and the victim but are mostly felt by the victims. Dark psychological abuse tends to mostly affect the victim emotionally; however, most times, it can be difficult for victims to identify signs of psychological abuse because they may be subtle, especially at first.

Dark psychological abuse has both short and long-term effects no matter how long or short the abuse takes place. For instance, experiencing narcissism tends to destroy your self-worth, sense of self, personality, and values. Experiencing constant narcissistic attacks might even cause you to drop your boundaries and allow the narcissist to control you.

The effects of dark psychology are numerous, depending on which type of abuse you experience or are currently experiencing. However, I will break down the effects of dark psychological abuse into three distinct groups, which are: cognitive difficulties, behavioral issues, and emotional problems.

Listed below are some of the general effects dark psychology might have on you.

Cognitive Difficulties

Experiencing dark psychological manipulations can affect your cognitive capacities. Some cognitive effect of dark psychology may include:

- Poor problem solving

- Poor abstract thinking
- Poor attention span or decision-making skills
- Poor concentration memory
- Confusion
- Nightmares
- Uncertainty
- Disorientation of time, place, or person
- Heightened or lowered alertness
- Hypervigilance
- Suspiciousness
- Intrusive images
- Increased or decreased awareness of surroundings

Behavioral Issues

Dark psychology does not just affect your cognitive faculties, it can have an effect on your behavior as well. Behavioral effects or issues caused by dark psychological abuse could include:

- Withdrawal
- Antisocial acts
- Inability to rest
- Intensified pacing
- Loss of trust
- Eating disorders
- Change in social interactions
- Loss or increase of appetite
- Hyperalert to environment
- Increased alcohol consumption
- Change in communication

Emotional Problems

Lastly but in no way the least, dark psychological abuse can negatively affect you emotionally and cause you emotional problems. The emotional effects of dark psychological abuse include:

- Fear

- Guilt
- Grief
- Panic
- Denial
- Anxiety
- Agitation
- Irritability
- Depression
- Intense anger
- Apprehension
- Emotional shock
- Emotional outbursts
- Feeling overwhelmed or fatigue
- Loss of emotional control
- Inappropriate emotional response

In addition to the aforementioned effects of dark psychological abuse, it is common for a victim of dark psychological abuse to suffer from what is known as Stockholm Syndrome – especially when the victim has been exposed to the abuse on a long-term basis.

The victim becomes extremely terrified of their abuser to the point that they eventually bond with them in an attempt to stop the abuse. In fact, a victim suffering from Stockholm Syndrome might even defend their abuser's abusive actions as they have become used to being abused. This is why it is sometimes difficult for people suffering from dark psychological abuse to leave their abusive partners.

Chapter 5: Signs That You are Being Manipulated

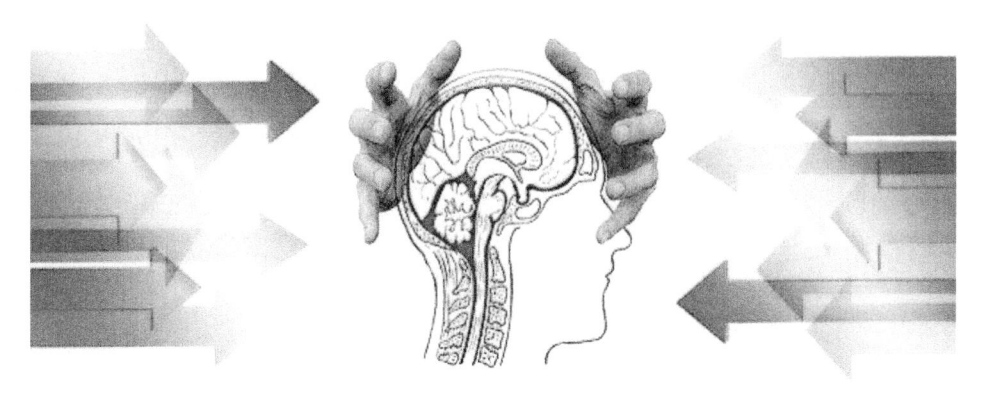

The signs that you might be undergoing or experiencing some form of manipulation are numerous and usually depend on the manipulation technique you are being manipulated with. Oftentimes than not, the signs of manipulation are not physical; rather, they are emotional and are sometimes hard to pinpoint. This is because manipulative experts know how to mask their manipulative practices to the extent of sometimes making themselves look like the victim when you eventually lash out. That is why sometimes, if you are asked to mention instances of manipulative abuse you have experienced, you might find it difficult to pinpoint a certain event that stands out to you.

That said, it is no secret that manipulative people can be found anywhere, as manipulation does not just occur in romantic relationships alone. A manipulator can be a narcissistic family member, a psychopathic friend, or a Machiavellian colleague at work. Hence, the signs that you are being manipulated by any of these people will vary according to their chosen manipulation technique.

Nevertheless, while the signs of manipulation might not be outrightly evident, there are still some warning signs that can signal to you that you are being manipulated. Being able to identify these warning signs will go a long way in helping you protect yourself from any form of manipulation.

So, what are these signs?

Let us take a look at some of them.

Warning Signs of Gaslighting

Signs of Gaslighting in Relationships

Gaslighting is a common form of manipulation that tends to occur in relationships. This is because, usually, there has to be some sort of intimacy between the abuser and the victim before any form of gaslighting can take place. This intimacy between the abuser and the victim is usually what contributes to the success of gaslighting as it would be difficult for a gaslighter to try and gaslight someone they share absolutely no form of intimacy with.

Gaslighting usually takes place in a romantic relationship as one of the tools of gaslighting is love. Gaslighters tend to exploit their victim's love in a coercive and sadistic manner that ends up making their victims believe that they are losing touch with their sense of reality. Interesting to note, gaslighting manipulations are more common the longer couples are together. Additionally, gaslighting can also be used as a coercive control tactic in a relationship – especially if the gaslighter is the primary income earner in the relationship.

As I mentioned earlier in this book, gaslighting is usually a form of manipulation employed by narcissistic individuals. Due to the lack of empathy on the part of a narcissist, they are able to systematically deceive their partners into believing that they are the source of all their problems as they go about criticizing, belittling, and abusing their partner with no accountability for their own faults.

The process of gaslighting is long and it usually progresses in stages. At the beginning of a relationship, the victim may notice that something uncomfortable is happening within the relationship but may be unable to precisely say what it is. Then, as time goes on, the victim becomes increasingly confused, worn down, and emotionally exhausted by their abuser's manipulative tactics, indifference, berating, and intimidation. Hence, this process tends to feed off of itself because as the gaslighting tactics weaken the victim's defenses, they become more vulnerable and helpless against continued abuse.

Listed below are warning signs or red flags that usually signals that you are being gaslighted in a relationship:

- A common warning sign of gaslighting is always thinking or assuming that anything that goes wrong is your fault.

- Apologizing often, especially when you feel like you have done nothing wrong is also a sign that you are with a gaslighter. A gaslighter always places their victim in a precarious position of automatically assuming that anything that goes wrong is the victim's fault. Hence, whenever something happens, a gaslighter will never apologize because to them, apologizing will make them look like they made a mistake. And believe me when I say no manipulative gaslighter ever wants to admit that they did something wrong. Even if they did, they would rather pin it on you than apologize for it.

- Another warning sign is wondering if you are being too sensitive to the actions of a person. In fact, this is one of the mantras of a manipulative person that is gaslighting their partner – they will often tell their partners that they are being overly sensitive.

- Having a sense or feeling that something is wrong, but being unable to pinpoint what exactly is wrong is also a warning sign that you are being gaslighted. It is common not to be able to pinpoint outright instances of gaslighting because of its insidious nature.

- Being more anxious and less confident than you used to be – especially when you are around the manipulator.

- Another warning sign that you are being gaslighted is feeling like everything you do is wrong. This is exactly how a gaslighter wants you to feel. In fact, it is their ultimate aim to make you feel this way.

- Making excuses for your partner's manipulative behavior. This is a side-effect of the Stockholm Syndrome I mentioned in the previous chapter.

- Feeling hopeless and taking little or no pleasure in activities you used to enjoy. This is usually a by-product of constant and long-term manipulations.

- Feeling isolated from friends and family. A gaslighter will usually try to isolate you from your family and friends so that they can easily submerge you under their manipulative practices.

Signs of Gaslighting in the Workplace

Although gaslighting is usually a type of manipulation that occurs in a relationship, it also has the ability to spread its tentacles to the workplace. The hierarchies of power and authority in the workplace usually provides a manipulative leverage for gaslighters.

Some workplace gaslighting behaviors may include the following:

- Stealing credit for your work and effort
- Not wanting to share credit on joint assignment
- Spreading malicious and slanderous lies about you around the workplace
- Pitting other co-workers against you
- Giving undeserved negative reviews
- Harassing or intimidating you at work
- Making you seem or feel incompetent in the presence of other workers

Just as in other contexts where gaslighting takes place, experiencing gaslighting at the workplace usually results in various problems for victims, such as anxiety, exhaustion, powerlessness, and the doubting of their perceptions.

Ultimately, experiencing gaslighting tactics or behaviors such as those noted above are highly detrimental to the psychological health of the victim. In fact, experiencing workplace gaslighting often makes victims apprehensive about going to work each day, makes them feeling alienated from their other co-workers, as well as make them feel unhappy and dissatisfied at work.

Workplace gaslighting has the potential to cause a high level of damage at both an individual and organizational level; hence, both employers and staff need to recognize warning signs and act as soon as possible to prevent the damage that comes with gaslighting at their workplace.

Signs of Gaslighting Children

Due to the vulnerability and powerlessness of children, they may also be targets of gaslighting tactics within the family system – especially by their parents.

Due to probably experiencing the same thing from their parents and thereby normalizing it, some parents might not know that what they are doing is essentially gaslighting and that it has a profound and terrible effect on their kids.

Parent might be gaslighting their kids by ridiculing them, causing them to feel worthless, or unloved either through harsh words or harsh actions, convincing them that they are not normal – especially through the type of words they say to them, comparing and contrasting them with other kids, and making them feel inadequate either through verbal or non-verbal means.

Coercive control and gaslighting by parents might appear in the following ways:

- Children may be forbidden from having friends in the home as a way of preventing others from seeing what is going on in the family.

- Parents may restrict their kids from participating in any social activities by giving them unrealistic homework and chore to complete.
- Parents might try to exercise control by isolating children from their friends thereby denying them from having supportive relationships.
- Just like the workplace gaslighting, parents may create resentment and tension between siblings by pitting them against each other by constantly comparing them to each other.
- Parents may prohibit their children from expressing their feelings or opinions, thereby creating a toxic environment.
- Some parents can stoop so low to deprive their kids of essential resources such as certain foods or technology.
- Making fun of their children or engaging in destructive teasing is also a method of gaslighting.
- Children may be blamed for any chaos within dysfunctional or abusive households
- Enforcing excessive rules and regulations around the house is also an example of gaslighting.

- Respect is reciprocal, demanding respect from their children with reciprocating it is usually a sign of gaslighting.

The abovementioned practices are some of the ways through which parents tend to consciously or unconsciously gaslight their kids. Besides being detrimental to the psychological health of the kids, long-term exposure to these gaslighting behaviors tend to make the kids normalize them and ultimately pass them down to the next generation. It is therefore important to break the cycle of gaslighting behavior before it extends its negative grasp toward more potential victims.

Classic Examples of Gaslighting

Besides the signs and examples of gaslighting in romantic relationships, in the workplace and in the family – especially when directed at children, there are other classic examples that might indicate that you are most definitely being gaslighted.

These examples include:

Trivializing your feelings: Gaslighters always try to downplay the validity of your feelings. They make it seem as if whatever you are feeling is not even worth talking about and that you are just making a mountain out of an ant-hill. They may even tell you that the reason you are feeling that way is because you are too sensitive.

Making you believe that people are talking behind your back: Another classic tactic that a gaslighter tends to use is by trying to make you believe that other people are starting to talk about you behind your back. They may go further by dropping some vague instances, but if you pay attention closely, you will discover that they are just trying to make you feel paranoid around other people. Their ultimate aim for doing this is to isolate you by making you start to stay away from people. You can call their bluff by telling them to tell you the names of the people that "are talking behind your back."

Denying their words to you: As part of a gaslighter's ultimate plan to make you seem crazy, they would often deny their words to you – especially things they said to you when no other person was around. They know that you have no evidence of them saying whatever you might be arguing that they said. Hence, the burden of proof is always solely on the victim's shoulder.

Hiding objects from you in a bid to make you look crazy: In a bid to further make you look crazy, a gaslighter will usually hide objects from you then pretend as if they had nothing to do with it. They may move your car keys and hide them in an entirely different location; hence, when you start looking for it, they may casually point it out to you and tell you that you are now in the habit of forgetting where you keep your stuff.

The above are just some examples of the insidious nature of gaslighting. The macabre thing about gaslighting is that it is usually difficult to prove as a gaslighter often knows how to cover their tracks. A gaslighter also knows not to try and gaslight you in the presence of another person – except the other person is in on it. Hence, most gaslighting tactics usually take place in private away from the eyes of other people.

Additionally, gaslighters are prone to using certain types of words when trying to gaslight a person. Thus, when you are being gaslighted by a person, you might hear them say the following:

- "You are overly sensitive!"
- "You are too emotional!"
- "You are simply imagining things!"
- "Can you even hear yourself, what you are saying makes no sense!"
- "You know you are sounding crazy, right?"
- "You are always making things up!"
- "That was a joke, stop taking things too personally!"
- "You are being too dramatic!"
- "You are making a big deal out of nothing!"
- "You are too paranoid"
- "Don't you think you are overreacting?!"

You might notice that most of the statements above begin with the word "you". This is because a gaslighter is an expert at identifying the supposed deficiencies in another person while hardly ever acknowledging or taking personal responsibility for the impact of their own statements or behavior.

Questions to Ask to Know if You Are Being Gaslighted

Listed below are some questions you need to ask yourself if you feel that you are being gaslighted.

- Do you feel that you are becoming unrecognizable?
- Do you feel like you cannot do anything right?
- Do you feel stuck or powerless in your relationship?
- Does the potential gaslighter regularly boast about themselves?
- Does the potential gaslighter frequently tell lies?
- Does the potential gaslighter fail to reciprocate the respect they demand from you?
- Are you constantly being told that you are too sensitive?
- Do you usually feel foggy and confused?
- Do you often second-guess yourself and your actions?
- Do you usually feel nervous, frightened, or anxious when you are around the gaslighter?
- Do you find that your feelings or thoughts are often trivialized?
- Do you feel like you are losing your self-confidence?

- Do you frequently experience indecisiveness?
- Do you find yourself doubting your memory or perceptions?
- Do you find yourself making excuses for the potential gaslighter?
- Do you feel intimidated or frightened by the potential gaslighter?
- Do you often feel like you are alone or like you have been cut off from your friends or family?
- Do you find yourself constantly taking the blame even when you did nothing wrong?

Answering "yes" to a greater number of the questions above indicates that there is a high chance that you are currently being gaslighted. Do not worry about this, in the subsequent chapter I will explain how you can protect yourself from being gaslighted.

Signs of Brainwashing

Obsessive: Brainwashed victims usually display extreme obsessiveness to a particular person or a group.

Dependency: Dependency on a particular person or a group for problem solving, solutions, and definitions without meaningful reflective thought is also a sign of a brainwashed victim. Also, a seeming inability to think independently or analyze situations without the person they are dependent on is a sign of brainwashing.

Blind Agreement: A brainwashed victim will agree unquestioningly with whatever their group or leader dictates, without any regard to the difficulty of following in lockstep or the consequences of doing so. In fact, for a brainwashed victim, anything the group or leader does can be justified no matter how harsh or harmful.

Isolation: A brainwashed victim will increasingly isolate themselves from family and friends unless they demonstrate an interest in the group or leader.

Withdrawal from life: Victims of brainwashing often seem withdrawn. They usually seem to lack whatever personality they possessed before they became brainwashed. Basically, it usually feels like they have become a shadow of their past self.

Signs of Hypnosis

The classic signs of hypnosis include the following:

Eyelids Fluttering: Usually, you will not be aware that this is happening. As you begin to get absorbed in the hypnosis process, particularly when you initially close your eyes to start the formal hypnosis, your eyelids will often flutter very quickly. At the same time or as a separate sign altogether, your eyes tend to move rapidly beneath the eyelids when closed. This eye movement is very common in individuals when they are hypnotized and asked to imagine certain visual things in their minds.

Physical Relaxation: Although you can be hypnotized without being relaxed, however, the quality of relaxation tends to be a characteristic many people have come to associate with being hypnotized. Very notable is the releasing of the facial muscles, which usually makes the subject look incredibly different; the jaw may also hang lower. This kind of relaxation is usually a sign that some sort of shift is occurring internally.

Pulse Rate Changing: Usually, at the beginning of the hypnosis session, your pulse may speed up as you enter the "unknown" with some level of apprehension. This especially happens if it is the first time you are undergoing the process.

Breathing Pace Change: As with the pulse, your breathing can fluctuate in the same way.

Subtle Twitching: If your body is relaxed, there may be some tiny involuntary spasms as you become hypnotized.

Catalepsy: This refers to the inability to voluntarily move your body or parts of it as a result of being so absorbed in the hypnosis process and experience. It is very rare for hypnotized people to move very much – if at all – while they remain hypnotized.

Altered Senses: While being hypnotized, it is not unusual to feel that your senses are altered. You might feel a sort of heaviness or lightness in your limbs. When hypnotized, some people become highly sensitive, and others the opposite.

These physical signs stated above are generalized; you may feel some or all of them. However, the moment you start to feel any of these signs, it is a sign that you are slipping into a hypnotized state.

Signs of Psychopathy

The classic signs of psychopathy include the following:

- Pathological lying
- Cunning and manipulative
- Lack of empathy
- Parasitic lifestyle
- Lack of remorse or guilt
- Glibness/superficial charm
- Need for stimulation/ proneness to boredom
- Poor behavioral controls
- Impulsivity
- Promiscuous sexual behavior
- Early behavioral problems
- Irresponsibility
- Juvenile delinquency
- Failure to accept responsibility for one's actions
- Criminal versatility – i.e., commits diverse types of crimes
- Grandiose sense of worth

- Lack of realistic, long-term goals

Signs of Emotional Blackmail

Here are a couple of signs that you might be dealing with emotionally manipulative people:

They are boastful in nature: Manipulative people are usually boastful in nature, as they tend to be very outspoken about just how wonderful they are. If someone seems to lack proper modesty as well as tact, that is usually a warning sign that they might be manipulative in nature.

They are self-centered: Emotional manipulators are extremely self-centered people. This is why they tend to make unreasonable demands from their partners without considering the opinions or desires of their partners. They tend to think solely about themselves without considering other people's feelings.

They are resistant to receiving criticisms and advice: Emotional manipulators hardly ever appreciate constructive criticisms about their manipulative actions. In fact, they tend to regard any advice given to them as an insult on their intelligence as they believe that no one can tell them how they should live their lives. Basically, criticizing an emotional blackmailer will do nothing except put you in their "bad book".

They tend to downplay the successes of others: Emotional manipulators cannot stand to have anyone look better than them; hence, they make it their mission to discredit the achievement of other people. They cannot bear to see other people succeeding and thriving – especially when they are not. Hence, if someone, probably their partner, achieves something, no matter how monumental that achievement might be, instead of being happy for them, they will find ways to disparage such achievement. Basically, emotional manipulators always want everything to be all about them.

Their mood is often unstable and volatile: The only time emotional manipulators are happy is when they are getting their way. However, the moment things are not going their way, the moment they encounter any form of resistance to their ideas, their mood tends to drastically change before you can blink your eyes. Emotional manipulators usually use their volatile moods to keep their partners on their toes as well as keep them in line. Most times, when an emotional manipulator's mood changes, their partners are usually pre-conditioned to try to make their mood go back to normal and the only way they can achieve this is by inevitably giving in to the manipulator's demands.

Other Indicators of Emotional Manipulation

When speaking of emotional manipulation, I believe it is clear that I am talking about a manipulation that takes place within a couples' relationship or between two individuals between whom there is a relationship and a very close bond. Hence, as soon as there is an actual manipulation, you might notice one or more of the following signs:

- Recurring nightmares
- Frequent feeling of bewilderment or confusion
- Little confidence in one's sense of reality
- Inability to remember the details of discussions with the manipulator

- Symptoms of anxiety: gastric disorders, tachycardia, chest tightness, panic attacks

- Fear or agitation in the presence of the manipulator

- Effort in telling yourself and friends that the relationship with the manipulator is fine

- Trying to avoid discussions with friends and relatives about your relationship with the manipulator

- Deep sadness

- Anger

Signs of Manipulation in Your Friendship

Here are a couple of signs of manipulation in your friendship:

Displaying passive-aggressiveness: Experiencing some sort of passive-aggressiveness from your friends is a sign that they are manipulating you. Some manipulators tend to avoid outright confrontation; hence, they usually resort to controlling their victims with passive-aggressive actions. Passive-aggressiveness is often used by friends who do not want to come across as being aggressive. Passive-aggressive actions include using ambiguous words, sulking, or giving you silent treatment, being overly critical of the people around you, or making sarcastic remarks. However, often times than not, passive-aggression might be difficult to pinpoint as the entire purpose of the behavior is to avoid directness while being covertly aggressive. An example of passive-aggressiveness is a roommate who is upset with their housemate for not offering some help with the chores around the house. Instead of confronting their housemate, they may start to tune out, ignore, or speak coldly towards that housemate while insisting that "everything is fine" if confronted about their passive-aggressive behavior.

Getting in touch only when they need something from you: Another way to detect if your friend is manipulative is if they only seem to get in touch with you whenever they need something. Friendship is not supposed to be that way, a friend is supposed to have a sort of presence in your life. If your "friend" is nowhere to be found when you need them to be your friend, but suddenly reappear whenever they need a favor from you, then such a friend is exhibiting signs of manipulation.

Asking a lot of favors without reciprocating them

Friends that manipulate you this way are always trying to gauge how far you will go in fulfilling their requests. These types of friends only become your friend because they feel they can easily get it on with you. At first, their requests and demands start small and you might not mind obliging them. However, as time goes on – especially when they see that you are always complying with their requests – they tend to start increasing the magnitude of their demands. And this is when it becomes apparent that you are being played. An example of this type of manipulative behavior can be seen in the following: David and Max are friends, and they make use of the same gym which is across town. Before they became friends, Max has always gotten himself to the gym without any issue, but the moment he became "friends" with David, he started claiming that he does not like driving. Since David did not mind driving, he usually goes to pick Max up from his house before driving to the gym. However, after doing this for quite some time, David noticed that Max started demanding that he drives him to other places – even suggesting at one point that David should drive him to meet his date! This was when David realized that his friendship with Max had been conditional from the get-go.

They never listen to you: One of the signs that your friend might be manipulative is if they always fail to pay attention to you whenever you are talking to them. For instance, if you feel that your friend is always tuning you out whenever you talk to them, while only engaging you whenever they are the one doing the talking then your friendship with them might be one-sided and manipulative in nature. This is especially true if most of the conversations you have with them are never about you.

They always want to be in charge: If your friend always wants to be in charge whenever making decisions, then they might be manipulative in nature. This is especially true if they tend to get upset if you suggest that you guys do things differently. When someone is unwilling to see your point of view, or they always think that their way is the best and right way, then they are most definitely manipulative in nature.

They are always defensive: A sign of a manipulative friend is if your friend always gets upset or defensive whenever you confront them about their manipulative behaviors. Usually, whenever you confront them about some of their behaviors, they become very defensive and resistant to even hearing out your perspective. A common tactic is for them to become emotional so as to divert your attention from the issue at hand. If you constantly feel like your concerns are not getting across to them, then you might be dealing with manipulation.

Signs of Manipulation in Your Relationship

Here are a couple of signs of manipulation you might come across in your relationship:

Picking petty fights: If your partner is always picking up petty fights with you – especially when you resist their demands, that is a sign that they are manipulative in nature. Manipulative people usually use this tactic as a controlling technique in a relationship. They believe that starting petty fights with you will ultimately make you give in to their demands.

They always put the blame on you: If your partner is always blaming you for things you did not do, this is a sign that they are manipulative in nature. They usually use this tactic whenever they want to get you to do something for them. They know that blaming you will make you feel bad and inevitably make you give in to their demands.

They are secretive in nature: A manipulative person constantly keeps secrets from their partners. They are extremely secret in nature but always want you to open up to them at all times. For instance, you might notice that your partner always moves out of the room whenever they want to take a call, or they tend to go to places without you, or they tend to do things without talking to you about it; however, if you do any of the aforementioned things, they tend to blow a gasket. Basically, they want privacy but will not let you have any. They always want to check your phone, but would never allow you to do the same. This is a sign of manipulation.

They tend to use you as a scapegoat: manipulative people never take responsibility for their actions, rather they will always find ways to pin their mistakes on you. For instance, your partner might forget to lock their car at night, instead of admitting that they made a mistake, they will find a way to blame you for it, possibly by telling you that they forgot to lock their car because you distracted them by talking to them.

They try to isolate you from your friends and family: In order to be able to fully manipulate and control you, a manipulative person will try to isolate you from people that care about you. They do this so as to become the sole controlling force in your life. A manipulative person knows that when you do not have access to the people that care they can easily manipulate you without fear of intervention from people that genuinely care about you.

They tend to take advantage of your kindness: Most manipulative people like to be close with people who are kind in nature so that they can take advantage of them. When a manipulative person realizes that you are kind in nature, they will try to take advantage of your kindness by constantly making excessive demands from you. They do not care if their demand might inconvenience you or might be difficult for you to achieve.

They tend to belittle you: If your partner is constantly berating and belittling you, they are most definitely manipulative in nature. They use this tactic to make their partners feel worthless and subjugate them under their influence. They subtly make you feel as if you are inferior to them or that you are beneath them or they might even make you feel as if you are nothing without them. They may even go as far as telling you that they were never interested in you but only got involved with you because you were available. Needless to say, this is a manipulative tactic to make you feel lesser than you are.

They constantly misinterpret your words: A manipulative person will always take your words out of context and misinterpret them to fit their own context. They do this to play mind games with you. They might try to put words into your mouth or completely twist an innocent comment you made to fit their own twisted imagination. They usually do this to pick up petty fights with you and wear you down mentally.

They make the relationship about themselves: Another sign of manipulation in a relationship is that the relationship always feels one-sided. In fact, sometimes, you might feel as if you are alone in the relationship. For instance, your partner may shun you if you try to talk about yourself or talk about how your day went. They might ignore what you are saying or try to switch the conversation to themselves, thereby making you feel as if your issues are incomparable to theirs.

They express passive-aggressive emotional behaviors: Displaying passive-aggressive behaviors like ignoring to talk to you about what is bothering them but choosing to do a particular action that they know will offend you or make you upset. They may make rude comments under their breath when they know you are close by or purposely leave a mess and expect you to clean it. For instance, after being confronted for not doing chores around the house, a manipulative person might exhibit passive aggressive behaviors by intentionally doing a poor job the next time they do the chores and when they are confronted about it, they will claim that they did their best.

They constantly rehash your mistakes: It is normal to make mistakes due to our human nature. When you make mistakes, normal people would forgive you and forget about the mistake; however, reverse is the case with manipulative people.

Manipulative people will always bring up your mistakes over and over again – especially when they fail to get their way with you.

They constantly bully you: If you are always being bullied in a relationship, chances are that you are with a manipulative person. A manipulative person usually comes off as mean, sneaky and may constantly use the threat of violence to make you comply with their demands.

Chapter 6: Protecting Yourself Against Dark Psychology

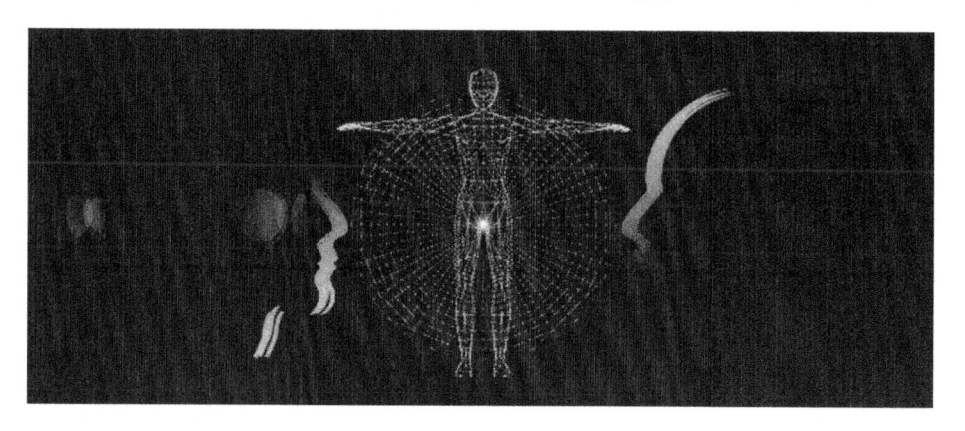

The preceding chapters have educated you on what dark manipulation is, the elements of dark psychology, the techniques of dark psychological manipulation as well as the effects of dark psychology. Hence, this chapter is dedicated to teaching you how to protect yourself against the various forms of dark psychology. To help you digest this information properly and easily, I will explain how you can protect yourself against the three major elements of dark psychology.

Protecting Yourself Against Narcissism

Although you might not be able to control or predict a narcissist rage, you can definitely learn how to protect yourself from its malevolent effects. Hence, through the ways discussed below, you can learn to combat the attacks of a narcissist before they wreck your sense of self-esteem.

So, let us get to it.

Realize that it is okay to protect yourself: The first step in protecting yourself from narcissistic attacks is to realize that you have a right to want to protect yourself. Regardless of who the narcissist is to you, regardless of how long you have been with them, you have to understand that wanting to protect yourself is not a bad thing.

You have to understand and believe that no one has a right to undermine your efforts, neither does anyone have the right to constantly make you feel sad, angry, or unhappy. You have to realize that you do not have to keep up with hurtful and malicious behaviors. Wanting peace and tranquility in your life is not a bad thing; hence you have to be prepared to fight for your peace. You have to keep in mind that no one but you can fight for your protection.

Learn to ignore the narcissist and their narcissistic actions: A narcissist favorite tactic is to draw you into senseless conflicts with them. When you engage a narcissist, you are automatically stooping to their level and playing their game. Since they are experts at their insidious games, you can never get the upper hand by engaging them. Reacting to their passive-aggressive behaviors or any other nasty tactics only pulls you into their malicious games, and that is precisely what a narcissist is always after. You might have heard the phrase "it takes two to tango", choosing to engage their narcissistic games means you are choosing to join in on their narcissistic dance. Hence, when they successfully draw you into their battles, they end up having control; and that control is the ultimate aim of a narcissist.

Therefore, the best option is to learn how to ignore them and their malicious tactics; learn to ignore their desperate attempts to demean you or otherwise draw you into their web of nastiness. You might have also probably heard the saying "misery loves company," this is especially true for a narcissist. Narcissists are naturally miserable people and they pursue any chance to force you to join their misery. Hence, when you are confronted by a narcissist, do not ever engage them, learn to ignore them totally. As a matter of fact, the more you ignore the narcissistic attacks of a narcissist, the less they tend to attack you – as they realize that "you are no fun". Conversely, the more you engage a narcissist, the more they tend to keep coming after you.

Refuse to take the bait: Sometimes, simply ignoring a narcissist is not enough as they will most likely start trying different tactics just to get a rise out of you – to get you to engage them. This is where your sense of resolve comes in, you have to make sure to continue to ignore any and all baits they throw your way. You need to regard a narcissist's bait as land mines. What do you do if you come across a land mine? Obviously, you walk around it!

A narcissist knows how to lay their bait like land mines, they lay them and patiently wait for you to step on them by engaging them. Hence, you have to learn how to avoid their baits, and you have to learn how to stand so strong in your convictions that the narcissist ultimately comes to the realization that they have no control over you and your life.

Do not take their baits and do not allow yourself to fall onto the land mines that they set for you. Even if they bring up old conflicts – as narcissists are prone to do – ignore them! Do not allow yourself to become a victim of their schemes – stop giving them the power to take away your sense of happiness on demand.

Define and maintain your boundaries: Setting and maintaining boundaries is very useful when you are trying to protect yourself against narcissistic manipulations. Hence, you need to take the time to expressively set your boundaries. Setting boundaries involves deciding what you are comfortable accepting and what you are not comfortable accepting and making it very clear to the narcissist. Naturally, narcissists dislike boundaries because to them it is a fence that keeps them from violating your peace and happiness – this is all the more reason for you to create those boundaries.

Think about what you are comfortable accepting and what you are not, take the time to consider the things you are willing to accept in your life, then take note of the things that cross the line for you. Take note of what you want from your life, as well as how you need others to treat you in order to enjoy your time with them, then combine all this to create a realistic boundary that would keep the narcissistic manipulator in check.

However, you have to keep in mind that it is not just enough to set boundaries, you have to consciously enforce them as well. When you feel that the narcissist is already overstepping their boundaries, make sure that you explicitly tell them so, and make it clear that you would not accept such.

Always follow through on your decisions: As I mentioned earlier, it is not always just enough to communicate your boundaries to a narcissist, you have to follow through by actively enforcing your boundaries. The only thing a narcissist understands is action, to them actions speak louder than words. Hence, it is necessary for you to follow through on the decisions you commit to whenever your boundary lines are crossed. While this is not easy, it is necessary for you to get assertive when you would prefer to let an infringement on your boundaries pass unanswered.

If you ever find yourself in confrontation with a narcissist, simply tell them the conversation is over, then walk away; do not give in to their persistent hounding or desperate plays to gain control over you. Follow through on the decisions you make and start sticking up for your own needs rather than always giving in to their injured sense of pride.

Keep in mind that you do not have to give a reply neither do you have to justify yourself. You do not even have to listen to them. There is no written law that says you need to entertain personal attacks from other people — regardless of who they are to us.

If you need space, get some space. If you tell a narcissist that another attack would result in you severing your relationship, do it, cut them off. Remember, your boundaries are only as good as the action you commit to protect them and a narcissist needs to be able to see that from a mile away.

Understand and accept that you are not responsible for the way they are: You have to constantly remind yourself that you are not responsible for the psychological disorder a narcissistic person has. You have to understand that their insidious and malicious behaviors are completely as a result of who they are and are not in any way related to you. You are not responsible for how a narcissistic person chooses to behave.

You need to accept the fact that the moment they choose to hurt you, they cease being your responsibility. You are not responsible for their hurtful actions, and you should not try to burden yourself by worrying that you might be the one causing them to behave the way they are behaving. A narcissistic person would want to blame you for their actions, but you should never accept any blame for their narcissistic actions.

The problems that a narcissistic person has are not your fault, and ultimately, they are not your problem. Having compassion for someone does not mean you should take on their pain and issues. You need to learn to detach yourself from their behavior and understand that all their lashing out has everything to do with them and very little to do with you.

Know when it is time to move on: Regardless of how much you care for a narcissistic person, you have to realize that narcissism is a psychological disorder that needs to be treated by a psychiatrist. Unless you are a psychiatrist, continually putting up with narcissistic attacks and manipulation have the potential to ultimately drain you and break you down. Hence, it is important to know when to let go of a narcissistic relationship.

Naturally, every relationship has its periods of ups and downs; however, when the "downs" start to outweigh the "ups" on a grand scale, it is probably time to move on from such a relationship. If you feel constantly manipulated, controlled, threatened, and abused in a relationship, it is probably time to protect yourself by leaving!

Protecting Yourself Against Machiavellianism

The best way to protect yourself against the influences of Machiavellianism is by learning about it – and I already explained what Machiavellianism is all about in chapter two. Hence, I will now be highlighting ways through which you can protect yourself from Machiavellians and their manipulative actions.

Establish boundaries and stick to them: Just like with any aspect of dark psychology, the first step in protecting yourself lies in establishing solid boundaries and enforcing such boundaries. I already discussed how to do this; hence, I do not need to repeat myself. However, the most important thing about creating boundaries is that you have to enforce them. Creating boundaries without enforcing them makes your boundaries meaningless. Hence, when creating boundaries against Machiavellians, you need to ensure that you enforce such boundaries or else they would not serve the purpose of protecting you from the manipulative actions of Machiavellians.

Accept the reality of their character and their behavior: It is in the nature of Machiavellians to be deceitful and manipulative. In fact, Machiavellians do not consider manipulating people for their own selfish gains as wrong – and so, chastising them from a moral standpoint never works.

Hence, you need to accept the reality of their manipulative character especially if they have ever tried to manipulate you. If you have ever been deceived by a person thrice, then that is a strong indication that they lack a conscience and they possess Machiavellian tendencies. Since deceit is the linchpin of conscienceless behavior, you need to accept the fact that such a person will never change. Hence, you need to accept the reality that that is the type of person they are.

Learn to manage your vulnerabilities: If you have noticed that you tend to always look for the best in people, you have to constantly remind yourself that Machiavellians tend to take advantage of people who always believe that everyone is good. If you notice that you tend to be overly sympathetic to people – especially people you do not know – you need to realize that a

Machiavellian thrives on exploiting sympathetic people. Basically, you need to be aware of anything that might make you vulnerable and susceptible to the manipulative actions of a Machiavellian and work to prevent that vulnerability from being exploited by a Machiavellian.

Resist trying to beat them at their game: It is our nature to think that we can outsmart certain people. While that might be true to a certain extent, it is almost impossible to beat a Machiavellian at their game of manipulation. Machiavellians are experts at their games; hence, trying to outsmart them will likely lead them to redouble their own efforts to manipulate you. Do not ever try to outmaneuver them, if you try to, you might end up paying more than you bargained for.

Establish win-win outcomes: Unlike narcissists, Machiavellians feel no need to prove superiority in their acts of manipulation. All a Machiavellian is after is to get a positive outcome for themselves; hence, if at all you want to give in to the demand of a Machiavellian, ensure that you also get a positive outcome for yourself as well. For instance, if a Machiavellian demands that you help them do their share of work, you can tell them that you would agree to their demand only if they also agree to do something for you. Most Machiavellian would accept this exchange as it would sound very logical to them. Therefore, establishing a win-win outcome for you and the Machiavellian is one of the ways you can protect yourself from being exploited by them.

Spend less time with them: Just like with any bad influence, the less time you spend around Machiavellians, the less they will be able to manipulatively exploit you.

Protecting Yourself Against Psychopathy

As you learned from a previous chapter, psychopathy is a mental disorder and people who suffer from it are usually amoral in nature. That means that a psychopath does not ever consider their malicious actions as right or wrong; hence, they have the capacity to do what some practitioners of dark psychology will consider as morally wrong. As a matter of fact, out of all the three Dark Triad traits, people that possess psychopathy traits are usually the most dangerous.

Listed below are a few ways you can protect yourself against psychopaths:

Run: Needless to say, the first step to protecting yourself from psychopaths is to run as far as you can from them. In life, you need to accept the fact that some people are bad news – as it is in their nature to be that way. This is especially true for psychopaths, they are simply bad news and once you start noticing the signs of psychopathy in a person, do your best to run away from such a person.

Set boundaries: Agreed, sometimes running away might not be an option you can afford. For instance, a teenager that lives with a psychotic parent might not be able to afford running away from such parent as they still rely on them for their welfare. In such a case, the next best way to protect yourself is by setting boundaries between you and the psychopathic person. Set those boundaries and let them know the consequences of overstepping their bounds. For instance, if you cannot run away from a violent psychopath, let them know that the next time they try to hurt you, you would call the cops on them.

Just as I mentioned earlier in the book, the most important aspect of boundaries does not lie in you setting them, rather it lies in you enforcing them.

Restrain yourself from arguing with them: Whatever you do, do not ever engage a psychopath in an argument. Engaging psychopaths in argument only serves one purpose: escalation. And because of the unpredictable nature of psychopaths, you never know what sadistic thing they will do once an argument with them gets escalated. So, instead of engaging them, simply leave the scene until they eventually calm down.

Protecting Yourself Against Gaslighting

The effectiveness of gaslighting lies in the fact that the victim does not know that they are being gaslighted. And this is because most people cannot discern the signs of gaslighting.

However, this is not an issue for you because I have written extensively about the signs of gaslighting in this book. Hence, the moment you start to notice signs of gaslighting from a person close to you, do not go into denial, trust your instincts, and protect yourself through the ways discussed below.

Record everything you can: The ultimate aim of a gaslighter is to distort your sense of reality up to the point you feel you cannot rely on your memories anymore. Hence, the best way to protect yourself against this is by recording everything you can. You can do this by keeping a secret diary where you record the day's events in your own words. Keeping a diary allows you to track events, including the date, time, and details of what happened. You can also take pictures as an additional proof of an event; this will help you to fact-check your memories and remind you that you are not imagining things even if the gaslighter claims you are. Also, you can try keeping voice memos, this is especially useful if you do not have the time or strength to write in your journal at the end of each day.

Recording these events are not enough, you have to make sure that you keep your recordings where the gaslighter will never have access to. You can even go a step further by sending copies of your recordings to a trusted friend or family member, so that in the event that the gaslighter finds your stash of proofs and destroys them, you can easily have a backup to fall onto.

Keep some distance and evaluate your position: Another way you can protect yourself from a gaslighter is by keeping some distance from them. Then, you need to evaluate if the relationship you have with the gaslighter is worth maintaining. If your relationship with a gaslighter is causing you more sadness than joy, you do not need anyone to tell you that you need to leave such a relationship. A relationship where your self-esteem as well as your sense of reality is constantly being attacked is toxic and is not healthy for you to stay in.

Create a safety plan: Part of protecting yourself from the insidious antics of gaslighting is to create a safety plan for getting yourself out of situations that are too overwhelming. Your safety plan can include having safety places and escape points; that is, places you can escape to whenever you feel a gaslighter is starting to get to you.

Understand that a gaslighter's behavior is not about you: You need to realize that gaslighting is not usually about the victim; rather, it is about the gaslighter's desire for power and control. By now, I believe you know that gaslighters are almost always narcissists. Narcissistic gaslighters lack self-confidence and they tend to be flawed and insecure about themselves; hence, in a bid to cover up for their insecurities, they try to try and control people around them. To them, this is the only way they can prove their superiority.

Hence, you need to understand that a gaslighter's gaslighting antics is not about you; rather, it is about their need to satisfy their own deep-seated insecurities. You may never understand their motives and personality, but you have to understand that their problem is not your problem and ultimately, you are not responsible for trying to save or change them.

Build up a support system: Dealing with the manipulative antics of a gaslighter can become too tough for you to handle on your own. Therefore, you have to have a support system in place to support you on days when you feel too exhausted to deal with your gaslighting problems by yourself. Your support system can include understanding family members or trusted friends or even a therapist. Sometimes, just having someone to talk to can go a long way in helping you deal with the psychological manipulations of a gaslighter. Additionally, getting feedback about your perceptions from your support system will help keep you from feeling crazy. Talk to them about your perceptions and ask for their objective observations. When objective people tell you that your feelings and observations are valid, you will find it easier to hold onto your own reality the next time a gaslighter tries to make you doubt your sense of reality.

Try therapy and/or counselling: Sometimes, especially if you have been dealing with gaslighting for a long time, you might find it difficult to keep shaking off its insidious effects. This is because constant attacks from a gaslighter tends to psychologically wear down a person. Hence, to protect your mental health, it is advisable to try seeking counselling from a therapist. You do not have to consider admitting your problems to a therapist, counsellor or even psychologist as a sign of weakness. These people are best equipped to help people like you who have to deal with manipulative people. In order to recover from the manipulative antics of a gaslighter, you need a professional to help you process your thoughts and feelings – and therapy is the best way to do that.

Protecting Yourself Against Brainwashing

The ultimate goal of a brainwasher is to destroy the logical, rational thinking part of a person so that such a person can become emotionally driven. What a person becomes emotionally driven about depends on what they get brainwashed on.

In order to protect yourself from being brainwashed, you need to know the various tactics brainwashers use to brainwash people. Knowing these tactics will help you realize the different ways you can fall victim to an act of brainwashing.

Understand that brainwashers target certain people: Not everyone can be easily brainwashed, but there are certain people that are easier to brainwash than others and these are the people brainwashers are constantly on the lookout for. Brainwashers tend to target people who are going through a difficult period in their lives. This includes people who have recently lost their jobs, people who recently went through a painful divorce, people who recently lost a loved one, people who are suffering from some type of terminable disease and so on. Brainwashers tend to seek out these types of people because they know that emotional barriers are down at that point; hence, it is usually easy to manipulate and brainwash such people.

To protect yourself from this, you need to be wary of any stranger that comes into your life during your lowest point. Oftentimes than not, such people come into your life with their own hidden agendas. They know they can easily get to you because people who are going through difficult periods in their lives usually have lower emotional defenses. Hence, if you are going through a rough time, it is better you find solace with someone that you know and trust, such a family member or a trusted friend than to open up to a total stranger who might not have your best interests at heart.

Be wary of people who try to isolate you: Just as I mentioned in a previous chapter, in order for brainwashing to be successful, it has to take place in a secluded and isolated spot, as it is virtually impossible for someone to brainwash you when you are surrounded by people who care about you.

By now you know that the modus operandi of brainwashers is to target people who are going through emotionally trying times. Hence, after identifying such people, the next step involves trying to isolate those people from people who care about them. Hence, you need to be wary of people who invite you to secluded spots away from people you know. If you realize that someone – especially someone you do not really know – has been trying to isolate you from people – especially when you are emotionally down – get away as fast as you can from them as they might be trying to take advantage of your emotional vulnerability.

Watch out for people who make an attempt to change your identity: As I mentioned in a previous chapter, in order for a brainwashing process to be successful, the brainwasher has to completely break down the victim's self-identity so that they can rebuild the victim in their desired image. Without breaking down the victim's identity, the brainwasher will find it difficult to proceed with the brainwashing process. Hence, you have to watch out for people who show signs of trying to replace your identity.

Watch out for people who try to make you join a group by all means: One of the tactics of brainwashers is to try to lure their victims into groups that operate on the same ideologies and values that they are trying to brainwash you into adopting. This is how brainwashers prime their victims for the ultimate brainwashing process. They know that once they get you to join their group or cult, you would be exposed to their doctrines and ideologies, and after this exposure, it is usually easy to begin the brainwashing process on you. All they have to do at this point is simply suggest that the group is "holding a retreat" in a secluded place.

Usually, it is easy for an emotionally strong person to withstand this tactic, but you know by now that brainwashers do not go after emotionally strong people, they prey on emotionally weak people. These groups are usually operated by charismatic leaders who have had years of experience in "converting people to their cause". And when you combine a victim's emotionally weak state plus the charismatic influence of a cult leader, you will discover that these victims barely stand a chance of resisting indoctrination.

Hence, to protect yourself from this brainwashing tactic, never accept to go to a cult meeting when you are emotionally down. Stay away from people who persistently try to get you to do this.

Know yourself: It is difficult for you to be brainwashed when you strongly know who you are and what you stand for.

Oftentimes than not, people who are going through identity crises are usually perfect victims for brainwashers. The more you know yourself and the more you staunchly believe in your values and ideologies, the less susceptible you will be to the influences of brainwashing.

Surround yourself with people who care about you: As I mentioned earlier, you can only be successfully brainwashed in isolation. Hence, you have to ensure that you do not isolate yourself from people who care about you. Naturally, isolation tends to lead to a lot of negative emotional feelings such as overthinking, and depression, and a brainwasher can exploit these negative feelings to lead you on the process of brainwashing. However, by surrounding yourself with people who care about you, it will be difficult for a brainwasher to get access to you – and brainwash you.

Protecting Yourself Against Emotional Blackmailers

Listed below are a few ways you can protect yourself against emotional blackmailers:

Make them accountable: Always call out an emotional blackmailer whenever you discover that they are trying to manipulate you emotionally. Emotional blackmailers are used to getting their way and they hardly get called out on their manipulative actions. Therefore, you have to learn to stand up to them and let them know that they make you feel uncomfortable and taken advantage of. They might try to deny that that was not their intention or that you are being too sensitive; however, calling them out would let them know that you are up to their tricks and this would make them think twice before attempting to do such in the future.

Develop a strong mentality: One of the ways to protect yourself from emotional blackmailers is to toughen your mental self. Do not allow their insults or outburst get to you, do not give them the chance to mess with you mentally. Adopt a position of mental indifference to their antics. The more you ignore their attempts at manipulating you, the more they will start to regard you as an impregnable fortress. And ultimately, when they see that they are unable to manipulate you, they will eventually give up trying.

Stop complying with their demands: You might have been giving in to the demands of an emotional blackmailer for so long that it now seems like a second nature. However, that is all in the past; moving forward, you need to stop complying to any and all demands that come from the emotional blackmailer. You have to realize that emotional dominance over another person is not love or friendship. You do not deserve to be constantly blackmailed emotionally. Therefore, you need to make the emotional manipulator understand that henceforth, you will be focusing on doing what is right for you and not for them. Regardless of whatever form of emotional blackmail they try, always maintain your stand.

Conclusion

Congratulations dear reader, you made it to the end of this book.

I believe that after reading through this book, you have learned a lot of useful things about dark psychology.

The information divulged here is not meant to teach you how to use dark psychology on the people around you; no, it is not. Rather, the information in this book is meant to help you understand the concept of dark psychology, its techniques, its nefarious effects, the signs that you might be undergoing some form of manipulation and, most importantly, how to protect yourself against dark psychological manipulation.

It is my hope that reading this book has helped you in one way or the other. If it has, kindly share this book with your friends and family so that they can benefit from the information inside.

Remember, everyone has dark psychological tendencies in them; however, what separates us from the rest is our strong resolve not to act on them. Keep spreading love to people, keep protecting yourself against manipulators, keep sharing information with others on how they can protect themselves as well.

Stay strong and never give in to any manipulator. If you find yourself starting to break down under manipulative pressures, do not hesitate to reach out to trusted friends and loved ones. Do not keep it bottled in, let people that care about you know what you are going through! Sometimes, just talking to trusted friends and loved ones can help you overcome anything you might be going through.

Harold Fox